THE NEW WORK
EXCHANGE

THE NEW WORK EXCHANGE

Embracing the Future
by Putting Employees First

SCOTT CAWOOD

CEO of WorldatWork

Forbes | Books

Published by Forbes Books, Charleston, South Carolina.
Member of Advantage Media.

Forbes Books is a registered trademark, and the Forbes Books colophon is a trademark of Forbes Media, LLC.

Printed in the United States of America.

10 9 8 7 6 5 4 3 2 1

ISBN: 9798887500263 (Paperback)
ISBN: 9798887500270 (eBook)

LCCN: 2022922815

Cover design by Danna Steele.
Layout design by Analisa Smith.

This custom publication is intended to provide accurate information and the opinions of the author in regard to the subject matter covered. It is sold with the understanding that the publisher, Forbes Books, is not engaged in rendering legal, financial, or professional services of any kind. If legal advice or other expert assistance is required, the reader is advised to seek the services of a competent professional.

Since 1917, Forbes has remained steadfast in its mission to serve as the defining voice of entrepreneurial capitalism. Forbes Books, launched in 2016 through a partnership with Advantage Media, furthers that aim by helping business and thought leaders bring their stories, passion, and knowledge to the forefront in custom books. Opinions expressed by Forbes Books authors are their own. To be considered for publication, please visit **books.Forbes.com**.

SEP 11 2023

Someone has to change the world of work. It might as well be us!

This collection of ideas, strategies, aspirations, and future thinking is for the World of Work!

Work is and always will be about possibility, exploration, and growth. Through work we connect and contribute to the world around us. Work is where magic happens.

To the WorldatWork membership: Your unwavering leadership, dedication, commitment, and expertise ensures that organizations perform at their absolute best by providing equitable rewards that make a critical difference to the millions of people who work.

The WorldatWork Foundation's scholarships, research, and initiatives build equitable and rewarding workplaces around the globe so that they can continue to make work better, and 100 percent of the proceeds from The New Work Exchange *go to the WorldatWork Foundation.*

AUTHOR'S NOTE:

A longtime practitioner of organizational optimization, communication, and relations, I have held many professional roles in human resources. I now proudly serve as CEO within an association that counts many human resources, rewards, compensation, and benefits practitioners among its members. Based on my background, at first glance, it might seem this book was written for organizational leaders or HR and rewards practitioners. However, my vantage point has given me insight into what people across the world experience at work every day—and what organizations could be doing better to meet the needs of people. This book was written for everyone who works as well as the organizations they are trying to thrive within.

CONTENTS

The State of Work

I love work. I've always been fascinated with the entire concept of how work unfolds between employees and employers. When I think about work, I think about opportunity. Work has never been about just *having a job*. From a young age, I felt drawn to work, not just for the earning but more for the ability to participate in the world. I wanted to experience the independence, fulfillment, problem-solving, and creativity of contributing.

Don't get me wrong. I'm *not* someone who'll tell you that I live to work or that life *is* and *should be* all about work. This book you've just picked up *isn't* about the work you know. Nor is it built on the antiquated Industrial Revolution ideal that people maximize their output for an employer as part of finding their value and purpose. I'm not here to deliver the message that if you are good to your company, then your company will be good to you.

Rather, this book is to signal our need to redefine work and workplaces as part of the *next* industrial age, which some call the Fourth Industrial Revolution.[1] Whether you are a leader in an organization who hires, sustains, and retains its people *or* a person who works within an organization of any kind, it's time to recognize and embrace the radical shift influencing *how, when,* and *why* we work—as well as *what* we produce. We're redefining work as both a concept and a practice. The exchange occurring between employer and employee is evolving right in front of us. There's a *New Work Exchange*™ emerging—these new paradigms influence our sense of purpose about work.

It's our job to work together as organizations and individuals to make work as rewarding, inclusive, engaging, inspiring, and productive as possible. In a world and within businesses that will always evolve, it only benefits us to try to *futureproof* our work as well.

> **In a world and within businesses that will always evolve, it only benefits us to try to futureproof our work as well.**

It seems like wherever we look, there are signs of change in the workplace. In many ways, we first see the changes through markers of discontent. That is, the news about work isn't all that great. Reports on "the state of work" read a bit grim. When was the last time you made it through a week without hearing about resignations, groups of employees striking or walking out to protest work conditions, or organizations scrambling for any kind of incentive to retain and attract people?

According to research done at my own organization, WorldatWork, nine in ten companies prioritized retention within the workplace in the twelve months leading up to March 2022.[2] Why? The same research study showed organizations experienced voluntary turnover well above the norms at 21 percent between early 2021 and 2022, with the turnover rate being more emphasized in the United States than in any other country.

While resignations will continue, they're simply an outcome of a larger problem. We need to look for the real root causes and hidden patterns to truly affect the outcomes with which we're unhappy. The pain points in the state of work are the tip of the iceberg. What's lurking under the water?

First, the workforce that existed before COVID-19 isn't today's workforce. The impact of the pandemic accelerated years of percolating social change. When people experience a shift, we bring change with us *into* our organizations and workplaces—and it can often take time for our institutions to catch up. Resignations are a symptom of that. The changes leading to resignations are the more pressing issues facing organizations. Organizations must change with the workforce.

Second, we have what I call a "caring problem" at work. Before anyone jumps to conclusions, I don't mean people have *stopped* caring. Rather, *what* we care about has changed. In Kenneth W. Thomas's book *Intrinsic Motivation at Work: What Really Drives Employee Engagement,* he writes, "Today's jobs are dramatically different from those of only a generation ago … jobs have changed so much that employees require a different kind of motivation."[3]

What's motivation at work? Work motivation is what we *care about* and the manner in which it drives how we engage in and produce our work. *Our priorities.* Leading up to the new millennium, there was a tremendous shift in how and why we worked as well as what we produced. Motivations evolved. The changes that have taken root in the past few years are no less radical—they just manifested quickly. The result is a lack of alignment between organizational and individual motivations.

As people redetermine their priorities, organizations have been unable to acclimate to what individuals *care about.* What happens if people suddenly care about different things than they did before?

What if organizations don't respond to the needs of their team? People don't feel organizations are meeting their needs and motivations.

In its *State of the Global Workplace: 2022 Report*, Gallup reported that 60 percent of people feel "detached at work." Even worse, the same report indicates 19 percent of the world's workforce is "miserable" at work.[4]

It seems like work has become the latest four-letter word. Why? It's the lack of alignment in what *we care about*. What are we going to do about it? If more than half our coworkers are detached and our organizations are weighed down by people unhappy at work, how are organizations going to respond? A lack of engagement and happiness at work, fueled by a lack of alignment in what we care about, prevents organizational growth, innovation, and productivity. In other words, our "caring problem" affects the organizational bottom line.

So how do people and organizations realign? As a person who loves work, I feel that's the question keeping me up at night. As a CEO, I myself want to fuel my organization's strategic growth by creating alignment within my team.

Let's be realistic for a moment: the topic of work is an easy target and at times a point of derision. People probably always have and will continue to complain about work. It's regularly the butt of jokes—whether in our conversations with friends or in hit TV shows like *The Office*.

I'm a huge music fan, and I often recall moments in my career by thinking of popular music from that specific point in time. Have you ever noticed how many songs there are about work? A quick web search provides a countless number of songs about "holding down a job," "working hard," and "leaving the workday behind." There are songs about work for every generation, and many iconic anthems aren't all that positive. Many of them are about trying to avoid work altogether. Laughing, talking, and singing about work seem like some universal ways we let off steam about the workplace. However, we're also clearly at an inflection point.

Let's go back to the data, which is a lot more serious than it's been in a long time. According to the same Gallup report, 44 percent of respondents reported experiencing stress "a lot" at work, 40 percent experienced worry, 23 percent experienced sadness, and 21 percent experienced anger. Those numbers are all *higher* than what was reported in Gallup's 2009 report, which was produced during the Great Recession when people were under tremendous stress. Of the respondents who admitted to feeling stressed at work, 49 percent claimed they didn't feel they were thriving or engaged at work.

At this very moment, how do *you* feel about work? How have your motivations at work evolved? Is your organization responding to and meeting your needs? If you are a leader or influencer in your organization, do you think your team is thriving and engaged? Or are there signs of detachment, misery, and misalignment? How does it affect you and your organization when the lack of alignment grows into a chasm and colleagues find it easier to quit their jobs rather than stay and influence change?

Work *is* one of the most important aspects of our lives—not just because it allows us to pay the bills or go on vacation but also because it helps us find identity and meaning. If emerging data hints at unprecedented levels of detachment and dissatisfaction with work, it begs us to pause and analyze some important questions:

- Where did we go wrong?

- Can we make work better?

The answer is a resounding "Yes!" To do so, we must embark on some radical changes in how organizations and leaders approach modern work. In many ways, individuals have already begun to redefine work for themselves, consciously and subconsciously. It's now time for organizations to listen, understand, and catch up.

According to LinkedIn, 90 percent of millennial and Generation Z employees report experiencing anxiety as the weekend draws to a close. Talk about dreading a "Manic Monday," as the Bangles did in 1986. But together, we can establish a groundbreaking new era when the idea of work doesn't give people a case of these "Sunday scaries."[5] We don't have to relish having our "real lives" during the weekends and fear the work week. It's time to put a lid on work-related "revenge bedtime procrastination" and get busy making work better. The New Work Exchange is understanding how we got here and mapping out our plans to get unstuck.

Across this book, we'll explore how work has been evolving for quite some time—and why the COVID-19 pandemic only accelerated and galvanized change in the workplace. As part of that, we'll look more closely at data about the state of work and analyze it as a disruptive opportunity. Things might look grim at times, but challenges are learning opportunities that can serve as differentiators in our organizations. Through the lens of overdue change, we'll assess how we can get back in the driver's seat to shape the changes we want and need at work. Practical, actionable steps that organizations and individuals can take at work will round out each chapter.

> **Have you ever just wished you could find more harmony in the relationship between your work and the rest of your life?**

Maybe you're here because you're wondering how to navigate the massive changes new technology and world events have brought to your industry. Maybe you've noticed the once-fundamental concepts of the office building and traditional workday are rapidly unraveling. Perhaps you are realizing you have a critical role in employee experiences—whether your role is to design, manage, influence, or improve relationships and culture. Or have you ever just wished you could find more harmony in the relationship between your work and the rest of your life?

Well, you're not alone. You're one of millions facing these questions, and I'm proud to count myself among you.

My whole career has been a process of working out the answers to these questions. While these questions may cause anxiety for others, I tend to geek out about finding the answers. In fact, I often describe myself as a "work nerd." My passion for learning about the workplace and how it functions (or not) inspired me to continue pursuing the topic in academic settings. Along the way, I pursued learning in organizational communication, labor and industrial relations, and education and my doctorate degree in organization and work-based learning. With an interdisciplinary foundation to understanding this thing called *work*, it's probably no surprise I translated theory and understanding into a passion for organizations dedicated to *great work*. With such a passion for work, I gravitated toward an organization that helps the world work better, WorldatWork, where—as CEO—I'm consumed with figuring out how to make work and the employee experience better for organizations across the world.

People are at the heart of every organization—that's something I witnessed and internalized at every stop in my career. I'm no stranger to issues of organizational culture, workplace dynamics, employee engagement, and workforce development. Before finding my way to WorldatWork, I spent two different stints in the unique and renowned work culture of W. L. Gore & Associates. I was also the vice president of global talent at both Revlon and the Great Place to Work Institute, which researches and selects *Fortune* magazine's 100 Best Places to Work. At one point, I joined a software company as its chief human resources officer and received an unexpected promotion when I was asked to take on the role of president.

Across these experiences, I've tried focusing on what I really love doing: helping people and teams figure out how they could be more effective. As a leader and as an employee, I've had my own personal experiences at both lousy and great places to work. All this experience has put me in a unique position to interpret the ever-changing nature of the modern workforce and to help employers—as well as employees—decode the new demands of the employment market.

In the face of all these changes, where do we go from here? Whatever our own roles are at work, how do we make work more valuable for everyone?

I'm glad you asked.

EMBRACING THE FUTURE

Together, let's map out our way forward into what feels like uncharted waters. We all have preconceptions about work that are starting to unravel—things we have accepted as fact but ultimately don't add value to the experience of work or to the success of individuals and organizations. Many of these ideas have served their place in the history of work, and we can be thankful they worked when they did, but they are now obsolete—or at the very least—need to be retooled.

Inside these pages, I invite you to move past griping and complaining about work to finding the solutions to make it better—for you, your team, your organization, and the world. Together, we'll identify the specific ways employment and business structures have shifted—and will continue to shift. We'll also review some actionable advice that'll help both you and your organization. We'll look at the direction of work and how it's becoming more human centric. Through the New Work Exchange, we'll not only survive the sea of changes but also take full advantage of the opportunities they bring along with them.

In this introduction, we've looked at the state of work, which is crying out for help and change. In chapter 1, we'll redefine work and explore the fundamental tenets of the New Work Exchange. This will help us move beyond approaching work *as a job* and embrace work as something that brings value to our lives *and* organizations. Then, in chapter 2, we'll examine how we got to our current state. We'll review the twentieth-century version of work, how it came about, and why we must understand the past work revolutions to influence changes today.

In chapter 3, we'll discuss why so many aspects of the work we've known have become obsolete, from the idea of the "corporate ladder" to the nine-to-five, suit-and-tie, five-day workweek. Chapter 4 explores the concept of leading people instead of *workers*. By shifting our perspective from transactional relationships with *workers* to building work experiences with *people*, we can be ready for real change at work. Chapter 5 covers inviting people within organizations to serve as real stakeholders. Finally, in chapter 6, we'll assess how to set a new pace within the workplace.

Across each chapter, I'll share personal anecdotes that bring these scenarios to life because this book is more than just theory—it's experience and observation from my vantage point of this work revolution. From my experiences, I'll also guide and recommend active steps to facilitate change.

The New Work Exchange is a philosophy, not a recipe or prescription for change, so successfully embracing a new approach to work will look a little different in every organization. For example, while some companies can and have comfortably moved to remote work or hybrid work models, only one-third of all jobs can be done offsite. You can't assume what works for you works for everyone.

At the same time, it's impossible to assume that what increasingly matters to you as an individual is in alignment with your organization. This New Exchange recognizes that alignments between people and organizations shift, so we all must be agile and adaptable because there's one thing we can't avoid: *change*. The changes we're experiencing aren't lamentable or accidental—they're inevitable. This is the next work revolution and the first step in understanding where work is headed is to understand where it came from.

Times are uncertain. But haven't they always been? While we like to say we're working through unprecedented times, every generation has faced uncertainty and adaptation at work. We've come a long way. We can learn from both the past and present of work to create the best possible future. To do that, we must manage ourselves and our organizations to be historically innovative instead of stuck in history.

In the words of author James Baldwin, "Not everything that is faced can be changed, but nothing can be changed until it is faced." A lot of times, when we say we want to see changes at work, what we really mean is we want others to change so our own lives are made easier. The data shows us we're past the point of waiting for others to make change happen. We all must engage to redefine our shared experience of work.

Work is collaborative and organizational, so our own perspectives, preferences, and actions must evolve. That's your fair warning that this book is for those willing to make real, lasting changes. If that's you, welcome aboard the New Work Exchange.

Now let's get to work.

CHAPTER 1

Working for Way More Than the Weekend

"What do you do?"

It's a question we've all asked—and been asked. It's a go-to icebreaker and marks the beginning of friendships, relationships, and opportunities. Work doesn't just explain what we do to earn a wage—it's an inherent part of who we *are* and is one of the greatest ways we can fulfill our purposes as human beings. Work can help us create value in our lives in addition to bringing value to others.

For such a short question, it packs a lot in it. Whether it's formal or informal, the reality is that most people do work, and many people love to work, but most of us also take for granted that work can be a total nuisance.

Throughout the introduction, we looked at the state of work. What if work didn't have to be seen as a four-letter word? What if we didn't approach it as a chore or count down the days to the weekend or our next vacation? What if by making it better and more meaning-ful, we could see work *add* value to our lives and organizations, have a positive effect on our happiness and engagement levels, *and* make money—for ourselves and our businesses—at the same time?

Maybe that sounds ambitious or naive, but throughout this chapter, we'll prime ourselves for the New Work Exchange by realizing that work can be more than a *job*.

Redefining work may sound too good to be true, but consid-ering the way many people see work in a negative light—and the overall impact of that—making work better isn't just a *nice to do*. It's a *need to do*. Influencing work is one of the most significant contribu-tions we can make to our own happiness, organizations, employees, customers—and, yes, the world.

At times, I sound like an idealist, but when it comes to work, I've seen what works and what doesn't. Looking at work through a new lens is the foundation of the New Work Exchange. While I don't expect every day at work to feel like a walk in the park, I am a firm believer that work can and must be a better experience—but that's not attainable if we continue to think about it as we do today.

Changing *how*, *when*, and *why* we work requires a new approach (mentally and physically) from all of us because we all shape our organizations, our own work experiences, and the work experiences of those around us. So to start, I'm going to share how my first experi-ences at work shaped how I think *about* work.

REFLECTING: WORK DOESN'T HAVE TO BE A JOB

When I was fourteen years old, I was eager to get to work. In my home state, this was two years too young to *legally* start working, but I wasn't going to let some pesky labor laws get in my way. I wanted to work, organizations needed me to work, and labor laws weren't a big deal to me at that phase of my life, so I assumed they probably weren't to others either. I also figured no one was going to check on a minor detail such as my age. Turns out I was right because while I was eventually fired from that job, it wasn't because of my age.

That's right. My first employer fired me. Let's explore why.

Like many teens, I entered the workforce through the world of fast food. All these years later, I can still recall the hiring manager's questions during my first-ever interview. Everything focused on logistic issues:

"What time can you get here after school?"

"What days can you work?"

"Are you going to trim your hair?"

Not a single question about me as a person. No discussion about the company's values, no debate to reveal whether I'd fit the mold of what they considered a good employee.

In my worldview, I've always been fairly innovative. I still like to find new ways to do things, and I was no different back then. However, as it turned out, that approach was in direct opposition to my employer, who was *very* prescriptive about process. There were rules for exactly how long we should cook fries and the order in which we assembled burgers. I had to memorize the order for putting condiments on the buns. You get the idea.

I, on the other hand, felt like we could improve the process and make it way more fun. So I'd take some extra time with the ketchup to draw a smiley face on the burger patty. Never mind that the customer would never see my innovative detail once the burger was delivered— surely they could taste the benefit of my personal touch. I'd hang out at the counter, chitchatting with customers, asking how their days were going—which of course, took up more time, leading to longer lines. Looking back, I guess I didn't quite grasp the concept of "fast food." Given the modern popularity of espresso art, I was just ahead of my time!

Long story short: I wanted to personalize the experiences and innovate in a place where they were quite happy with the way things were. They needed people who'd follow their rules and processes, meaning I was a terrible culture fit. So I was unceremoniously fired, which was probably the right thing for all parties. Even if I *had* been the right age, I probably never should've been hired in the first place. Interview questions were designed to demonstrate whether I *could* do the job, not whether I was a *good fit* for their approach, which is an important lesson I still carry with me.

This experience also introduced me to thinking of management as *them* and the employees as *we*, which meant I began to see the work as a *job* instead of something that would push me to be my absolute best. Decades later, I realize that the New Work Exchange requires us to find and build great cultural fit, requires us to understand that *us-versus-them* leadership is damaging to organizations, and should inspire and fulfill people as much as possible.

My next work experience—also in fast food—taught me yet another lesson I still see play out in organizations today, especially regarding how managers learn to lead people. Before I started at this new job, there had been an incident in which a former employee stole the polyester shirt that we all wore as part of our uniform. The manager's solution was to institute a rule that no employee could take home their work shirt. We had to leave our shirts at work, where they'd be waiting for our next shifts. As you can imagine, it didn't take too long for my shirt to get pretty grungy. After all, when you're working next to fryers, flipping burgers, and making hot fudge sundaes, it's bound to happen.

Then one day, the owner of the store came in and said, "Hey, you're doing a great job, but you've gotta wash your shirt." To which I responded, "Oh, I'm not allowed to take it home to wash it."

She was thrown for a loop. "What are you talking about? What do you mean you're not allowed to wash it?" It should be obvious that in a business where you're handling food, employee hygiene should be more important than losing a $15 shirt. Trying to fix a problem, the manager implemented a policy that created many more problems than the "solution" addressed.

I didn't stay in fast food forever. That was probably best for me *and* the fast-food industry. Still, these experiences have stuck with me my entire career, paving the way for my own journey of helping organizations reassess and adjust their work cultures. My examples happened many years ago, but they exemplify issues we still encounter in various forms at work today and prevent alignment between people and organizations.

It's easy to become blinded by policies at work, even when they are our own. As we look for universal solutions, they often become damaging to culture and very annoying to employees. Confusing policies often become reasons we end up working to get to the weekend or our next vacation.

> **We've come a long way but not far enough. To this day, managers and organizations don't always think of the wider implications— to the business and its people—of their decisions and policies.**

We've come a long way but not far enough. To this day, managers and organizations don't always think of the wider implications—to the business and its people—of their decisions and policies. Why do we get so stuck on a specific process? Why do managers build rules around one bad example and then apply that to everyone? Why do we insist on *one* right way of doing things? Instead of exploring and finding new paths, we spend a lot of time *making work a job.*

INFLUENCING THE WORLD AT WORK

Since my very first job, I've seen myself as a student of work culture. The common thread across my career is that I feel best about work when I'm helping people figure out how they can be most effective. After decades of experience at several organizations, my focus on effective workplaces took me back to the unique culture at W. L. Gore & Associates to head up their global organizational effectiveness team.

Feeling most at home at Gore, I had no intention of going elsewhere again. But it felt serendipitous and appropriate to receive a call that helped me explore new paths. One evening, I was out walking my dogs when I got a call from one of the board members of WorldatWork. When I answered the phone, he asked, "Hey, what are you doing?"

Thinking this was a literal question, I answered, "I'm currently wrangling a Great Dane and two whippets on the snowy streets of Delaware."

"No," he said, "I mean, what are you doing for work? I have a great idea of how you could influence the way work is happening around the world."

As he told me more about the history of WorldatWork, I was intrigued and realized how we could be an influence on work and workplaces. From my previous roles, I was already familiar with the association, which serves and rewards human resources professionals in organizations across the world. The conversation got me excited by the prospect of joining WorldatWork to map out strategies and concepts designed to impact the experiences of working people.

Six months later, I packed my bags and headed to the Arizona desert—in the middle of summer. It wasn't ideal timing, but it gave me a good excuse to stay indoors and get acclimated with the organization, get to know the team, and give the team a chance to get to know me. This included all the typical grill-the-new-CEO questions you'd expect. It was surprising when more than one person asked whether jeans on Fridays would still be allowed.

I answered all questions honestly and transparently, emphasizing that I wanted us to work on things that would elevate our game and set people up to do their best work. I added, "For some, that could mean you want to wear high heels at work, while for others, it's high-tops." That was the first of many shifts in the organization. It's worth noting that a handful of years later, our team is almost entirely remote, and "office wear" is a lot more casual than jeans on Friday. That's the speed and flexibility of the New Work Exchange.

But on a more serious note, I got busy focusing on the two agenda items that keep most CEOs awake at night: growth and people. Not to say there weren't other items on the agenda, but these are the two areas that provide the greatest opportunity—while also posing the greatest challenge. I wanted to create alignment between what my team cared about and the organization's focus. We started assessing what mattered to people and what mattered to our association members. We unpacked how we did things and how we could do them differently—then we applied those lessons to help our members discover different strategies for themselves.

Making an organization a great place to work means things must be great for both employees and employers. Those two things can't be mutually exclusive—if you make things better for one, they must improve for the other. There must be alignment, so figuring out what makes workplaces better for both the employee and employer is the key to good culture.

> **Figuring out what makes workplaces better for both the employee and employer is the key to good culture.**

Once I did a speaking engagement at which I had the privilege of following Jim Collins, who had spoken about his influential bestselling book *Good to Great*. In my session, an audience member asked, "Does the 'great' include the need for the people experience to be great?"

Since Jim was still in the room—and the question was about his book—I punted the question to him. His answer was simple: "This is way more than common sense—you don't get to great without creating something great for your people."

Well said, Jim.

Every day, all over the world, people work. Some love it; some don't. Nearly all work and workplaces can be improved—which not only helps organizations perform at their best but also helps the world perform at its best so all of us can have the lives we are chasing.

There isn't one corporate goal, board mandate, consumer buying trend, or employee experience that wouldn't directly benefit from rethinking our approach to work. Each day, billions of transactions happen in business, and to make them happen, organizations rely on *people* who work. I love the exchange that happens when someone has something to sell and someone else sees more value in acquiring it than holding onto their money. This exchange funds what we do in the business world and how organizations grow. However, the ongoing exchanges we have with our people underpin business success. People are at the core of organizational success, so we must prioritize opportunities to shape, influence, and redefine the exchange for positive outcomes.

There's an employee exchange taking place right now in your organization. Do you know how your team feels about it? Do your team members and organization care about the same things? The data we've looked at so far implies there's room for improvement on all fronts. So I'm asking these questions not as a judgment but as a call to action—for ourselves, our organizations, and the larger world at work. It's time to make work and workplaces better.

ALIGNING PEOPLE, BUSINESSES, AND ORGANIZATIONS

While work is the way we all earn livings, it can also be a measure of our influence on the world. It's tempting to see work as drudgery, leading many to adopt the infamous 1980s mantra from the song "Working for the Weekend," by the band Loverboy. However, we can't ignore the fact that work can add incredible value to our lives.

For most of the past century, work has mostly been an exchange in which an employer would essentially say, "Give me forty years of your life, and if you work hard, you'll get a paycheck to fund your life." However, the past few years have shown that work isn't *just* about monetary compensation. It's not just about the physical work*place* either. Instead, it's also about the value alignment between employer and employee. To take a bold step further, work is also about whether organizations can neatly design work to fit *into* the lives people need and want to live.

The New Work Exchange requires us to reassess and redefine the relationship between people and organizations. We must elevate the human element of work. Compensation isn't the sole currency between employers and employees. Unlike what we are often told in traditional business schools, salary plus benefits and an occasional company picnic *doesn't* equal a happy and productive employee. Instead, value alignment motivates our best work.

Ultimately, organizations are trying to find people who care about their work—and people are trying to find organizations that care about them and support what's important to them. It's a wonderful thing when the two find each other—and when it doesn't happen, when there's a break or gap between the two, then we inevitably run into issues as well as lose value and opportunities.

There's no prescriptive road map or specific sequence to create alignment. Focus on what's authentic to you and what will resonate within your sphere of influence. We'll explore some of these concepts more deeply in later chapters, but the following tips will get you started with finding alignment.

DISCOVERING WORK CAN BE DIFFERENT—IT CAN BE BETTER

Sometimes we can be so averse to disruption that we overlook how change can make things better. Complacency is expensive for both organizations and individuals. For people, it's time to sit down and determine what motivates and sustains you in this emerging new world. What are your priorities? What boundaries do you need to set or reset so you can thrive with your established priorities? Last, are you approaching work through any outdated tropes that are holding you back? If you approach work as *a job* but you still expect more from work, then it may be time to analyze whether your mindset is creating constraints.

Individuals aren't alone—or they shouldn't be—in assessing these questions. Organizations are made up of *people*. External change has been widespread for several years, so as part of the New Work Exchange, people within organizations must work through these questions and look to managers, leaders, and influencers to have constructive conversations on these topics. No one needs to work through these things in a silo. Having these conversations will counter people who feel disengaged and unmotivated. So think through your priorities and prepare to have conversations about them *at work*. We can't think our way into something better, so plan to have conversations *and* take actions that lead to change.

Organizations everywhere should welcome and take full advantage of inevitable change. People around the world have evolved through the pressures of the past several years—our organizations must also keep up.

Now let's flip the script and focus on organizations for a moment. Organizations that cling to the outdated view of work will gradually find themselves unable to compete for highly talented employees. In this modern era of work, organizations that start doing things differently will make work and workplaces both stronger and better.

Organizations everywhere should welcome and take full advantage of inevitable change. People around the world have evolved through the pressures of the past several years—our organizations must also keep up. Each change brings challenges and opportunities. We can divorce ourselves from outdated systems of work and transform work into something more meaningful for the people within our organizations.

UNDERSTANDING THAT PEOPLE ARE
THE CORE OF EACH BUSINESS

When businesses have thriving work cultures, there's usually a common attribute: they embrace that people *are* their business. In the Old Work Exchange, we traditionally defined work as what we "do," so we allowed the products or services rendered by our organizations to define us. In that approach, people are a means to an end, part of a machine and easily replaceable. It's time we let machines be machines—they *are* replaceable.

People are *not* machines, so why not build a way of working that lets us be the best people we can be? If we—by that, I mean individuals at work and organizations themselves—all put people back at the core of our businesses, then we radically reframe work experiences. Massive changes in workplace culture, compensation, and hierarchy have already arrived at many organizations. If they haven't arrived at yours yet, then they're on the way—and they all relate to putting people first.

In the Old Work Exchange, we gauged an individual's success based on things like quarterly numbers, profit, margins, and so on. These things will always be important for an organization's balance sheet, but on their own they can dehumanize team members by turning their contributions into a two-dimensional chart. When we see people as our business and want to improve their experience, it allows us to shift the conversation and focus on what it takes for people to do their best work.

CREATING A HEALTHY CULTURE THAT SETS PEOPLE UP FOR SUCCESS

Culture is the ultimate example of people and organizations coming together to set tones, approaches, and models for everyday business. A 2021 WorldatWork research study found that culture is a strong driver of employee tenure and that the right culture and personality fit is more likely to foster employee commitment.[6] There are few topics at work as complicated as organizational culture. It's a very layered construct that we'll discuss more deeply in later chapters. But to truly unpack culture's role in the New Work Exchange, we all must analyze how we contribute to, shape, or uphold team-based and organizational culture.

When business leaders are navigating cultural changes at work, which should include looking at policies and processes, a simple question goes a long way: "Does this help a person's ability to do their best work?" It's a simple concept and question but one that both people and organizations often forget to ask. There's a classic Peter Drucker quote: "Most of what we call management consists of making it difficult for people to get their work done." Culture is all about "how things get done around here." That manifests as policies, processes, mindsets, interactions, and decisions.

Think back to my manager with the "Don't take your shirt home" rule. Does my experience make you think of decisions made by former managers you've had? Does it make you think of decisions *you've* made? Does it make you think of "It's just how we do things here" policies at your organization? Organizations and the people at their core often spend too little time examining which rules *contribute* to success and which ones *prevent* success.

Change is a challenge for individuals and organizations. The desire for change isn't enough. Behaviors need to change. Decisions need to change. At work, that requires intersectional change organizationally *and* individually. We've got to be willing to unlearn, relearn, and let go of a lot of things we think we know about work to create something new for ourselves.

ESTABLISHING PURPOSEFUL CHANGE BEFORE THINGS ARE BROKEN

You're probably familiar with the famous John F. Kennedy quote "Change is the law of life. And those who look only to the past or present are certain to miss the future."[7] You're also probably familiar with the notion that you can't make change just for change's sake. There's much truth to that. But it's equally true that we can't resist change to avoid it. Refusing to change isn't the path of least resistance—it's a path to roadblocks.

Purpose should drive our changes. When things are *obviously* broken, most people and organizations are driven to change. At that point, change is also twice as hard. The real challenge is discerning when things aren't necessarily broken but are no longer the best way of doing things. We develop blind spots because a lack of awareness prevents us from seeing a better way.

You may be surprised by how much the "If it ain't broke, don't fix it" mentality exists in your day-to-day approaches to work or the processes within your organization. That's why I keep a piece of frayed rope in my office. It isn't really "broken," but if I were counting on it to keep me from free falling off a mountain, I'd certainly get nervous. That rope is my reminder to look for what's frayed. We need more of that in our personal approach to work and our organizations. In the New Exchange, we know *when* and *how* to change things *before* they are fully broken.

CHANGING THE WRITTEN AND UNWRITTEN RULES

The world should be a great place to work. The more productive, committed, and inspired we are as a workforce, the more people on this planet will thrive. To thrive at work, individuals must align with their organization's values. For people to know what their organization "stands for," company values have got to be clear.

I'm not talking about the savvy-sounding "values" an organization has listed on a website under the "About Us" section. I'm talking about what organizations *show* is important through policies, procedures, and processes that impact people, their work, and how they feel about work. Without a doubt, values are cultural drivers. We think of them as fixed, stationary items—however, values adapt and change in relation to priorities and *what we care about.* Values inform and establish day-to-day actions and decisions for individuals and organizations. Often hard to pin down, we sense or gain impressions of values by how they translate into *rules* at work, which are both written and unwritten, formal and informal.

> To thrive at work, individuals must align with their organization's values.

THE WRITTEN RULES

Organizations are full of written rules that have a direct impact on a person's ability to succeed in their role. Many are captured in handbooks or policies setting standards and expectations. Such rules are meant to be followed consistently across organizational functions: dress codes, expense protocols, email signature protocols, and even ways to set and conduct meetings.

Another permutation is something we refer to as *best practices* that organizations document and build into processes without questioning them. For example, *hiring for culture fit* has long been an adopted practice. This approach is often embedded in interview forms and internal-facing recruiting documents. The approach has become so widely embedded that it's no longer a philosophy but a rule and value that *we must uphold.*

The culture-fit rule begs an important question: If we only hire for culture fit, don't we just end up getting more of the same type of people? That is, when we hire *for fit,* aren't we really saying "We only hire people like us"? Instead, we should always be hiring for culture *adds*, not just culture fits.

Returning to the story of my first job, I think we can all agree I wasn't a culture fit, but was firing me really the best solution? Did I follow the written and well-established rules of conformity demanded by the organization? No. While the fast-food business model demands uniformity, I'm going to go ahead and use the example to make a point that applies well beyond the fast-food industry. What if instead they'd asked, "Where would Scott's skills be put to better use? How can we leverage what makes him different?"

Like many workplaces today, the employment exchange at my first job was heavily weighted toward what the *organization* needed— even if it created challenges for the employees. Sometimes we hire the wrong person, and they just don't work out. It happens to everyone. However, could the management have leveraged my skills to achieve more value and get better engagement out of me rather than trying to force-fit me into their preexisting ways of working? Could I have been a culture add who helped them reconsider some *written rules*? I guess we'll never know.

Inevitably, culture itself must evolve. For culture to evolve, our written rules must change. Just because something was productive, healthy, or helpful last year doesn't mean it'll remain so. If you had asked me a few years ago if I thought most companies would be interviewing, hiring, and onboarding staff digitally without candidates even stepping foot in a physical building for a face-to-face meeting, I'd have thought you a bit of a shortsighted renegade.

Over the past few years, we've seen a movement toward a more human-focused element at work. We're all (organizations and individuals) learning how to be more responsive to and accepting of colleagues' different situations. This includes more lighthearted aspects like guest appearances by a coworker's barking dog or snacking toddler during video meetings. Labor shortages across almost all fields fueled and emboldened people to be more transparent during the workday, leading to a blending of work and home life.

Consequently, written rules—like a strict company policy of working nine to five, five days a week—had to bend. Such a rigid structure didn't work for a lot of people. Organizations heard a lot of statements to the effect of, "These rules don't meet my family's needs and don't allow me to bring my best self to work." And so we've seen a shift in companies willing to experiment with allowing employees to choose their own schedules or move to a varied work schedule.

The written rules most companies have adopted over the past few decades often don't fit the range of issues we're seeing today, and that's a tremendous hurdle organizations need to clear for their own progress. Most of our current workplace systems (which lead to rules) are at odds with *people being people*.

As top talent pursue their life goals, they *can and will* find organizations that align with their priorities. People are increasingly less willing to accept the mediocrity of bad managers, one-sided rules and policies that only benefit the company, and executive misalignments around things like where, when, and how they work. Consider the rules at work—again, both the rules you set and the rules you follow. Could they benefit from some analysis and adaptation?

THE UNWRITTEN RULES

Likewise, we should all be assessing the rules we have at work that are in place but *not written.* It's easy for companies to say one thing in messaging and then have practices or policies that communicate something very different. These are often an organization's *unwritten rules*—discrepancies and inconsistencies in messaging that increase disengagement and ultimately end up decreasing trust.

One day, I was visiting an organization that was interested in becoming a better place to work. I arrived at their building and sat in the parking lot for a bit, just looking around. When I'm trying to gauge an organization, I always like to arrive at the workplace early to see things before anyone knows I'm looking. Sneaky? Maybe. But very effective. An early visit to a location was how I discovered that a hospital in Connecticut played soothing music in the parking lot to help calm patients and visitors, knowing most visits to hospitals come with a hefty dose of anxiety.

No soothing music played in the parking lot when I visited this particular manufacturer hoping to reach the ranks of great places to work. I watched as the morning-shift employees entered the building, and each employee underwent a search to even get *into* the workplace—backpacks and purses were sifted through and searched. Then, as the night-shift employees left, the same thing happened— burly security guards searched them too.

Finally, I decided to go in, wondering if I would have to lift my hat for Carl the security guard like I had seen employees do on their way out. No search for me. As I made my way into the building and started to walk down the hallway, I noticed two huge placards. One captured the company's history—marking various milestones and showing pictures of smiling founders—and the other really caught my eye because it spelled out the organization's five core values. The number one core value? *Trust.*

"Huh, that's interesting," I thought.

During my appointment with the general manager, I couldn't help myself. I said, "Hey, I noticed your five core values on the way in. Number one was trust. Number two was integrity, then teamwork. Now, are those the core values that are really guiding your culture? Do you think those five things drive the behaviors here? Do people feel connected to them or guided by them?"

"Yeah, absolutely. That's exactly who we are," he answered.

To which I replied, "Well, you're searching people as they come in and out of the building, yet you're saying trust is the number one value. That's a very inconsistent message."

We got into a bit of a debate about this, and I finally suggested it'd be better for him to take a black marker, cross out the word "trust," and instead document that their first value was actually "antitheft." Trust is a perfectly fine thing to value—however, we create issues when we say one thing but follow something else.

Another time, I was visiting an organization that rather enthusiastically showed me an invitation to their annual Employee Appreciation Day. Given their tenacity in showcasing their efforts, I jokingly replied, "Wow, a whole day for appreciation. Don't go overboard or anything."

To be fair, it did sound like a fun day. Bagel delivery to every team in the morning, a special message from the CEO, and then a team lunch featuring beers from around the world and cheeses from across the United States. After lunch, everyone got to end the day early. But what caught my eye the most was an asterisk at the bottom of the invitation reading, "See your supervisor for a ticket. Cost: $15."

When I sat down to talk with the HR leader giving me the tour that day, I couldn't help but ask about employees paying to attend their own appreciation events. "Hey, love the beer and cheese concept, the inclusivity and diversity of foreign brews and all that good, fun stuff. But what about this fifteen-dollar ticket? Is that if they want to bring a guest along?"

"Well, no," she replied. "The employees are funding this, so they have to pay for it."

You read that right. The employees were funding Employee Appreciation Day. As that thought sank in, I joked, "Next, you'll tell me it's mandatory."

"Well, it *is* mandatory," she admitted. "Everybody must go. But we've made it easier this year by allowing them to have the ticket price automatically deducted from their paycheck."

There are always reasons for *unwritten rules* creeping into our workplaces, culture, processes, and overall organizations. However, it's critical we analyze actions that aren't in alignment with what we claim to be important. Otherwise, those decisions often become inconsistent messages within organizations.

WALKING OUR TALK TO CREATE ALIGNMENT

No one likes to be called out on stuff that's leading to a lack of engagement, discontent, or less-than-ideal culture. But there's a common thread to creating alignment. What I call the *discovery of disconnect* involves uncovering and changing what's holding back our organizations. Quite simply, we can't align if there is a disconnect. Discovering a disconnect can be painful. The first steps of change create pain. But it's part of establishing a new approach to work.

We spend a lot of our lives working, so no one wants to despise work. It's possible to move beyond the paradigm of working just to get to the weekend. That requires organizations and people to *care about* and prioritize the same things. Alignment is established when disconnects are addressed. Remember the Baldwin quote I mentioned in the

> **The first steps of change create pain. But it's part of establishing a new approach to work.**

introduction? For things to change, we must face them first. A new order to anything takes work.

One of my favorite *discovery-of-disconnect* moments happened during yet another visit to an organization trying to become a best place to work. I was in the employer's cafeteria, getting a drink while I waited for my next meeting to start. On one of the walls, there was an oversized poster with the phrase "Dance like nobody's watching." Then I saw something stuck to the wall right next to the poster. When I walked over to see what it was, I couldn't help but chuckle. It was a security camera, which I think makes it a little harder to dance like nobody's watching.

Was this intentional? Probably not. But the goal is to *intentionally* reinforce—not obstruct—messages delivered to people at work. We need to intentionally find ways to help people believe, not distrust.

People want to believe what they hear at work. Organizations want to be credible and trustworthy. Such values underpin motivation and alignment. This new era of work requires that we regularly ask ourselves, "Can they believe me?" Without a positive answer to that question, there's limited possibility for alignment and limited opportunity to move forward.

CHAPTER 2

Looking Back and Moving Forward

W e've talked about the importance of alignment between people and organizations, and we've outlined how starting the journey toward the New Work Exchange requires that we shift our perspective on what work *is*. In this chapter, we're going to look back at some historical structures of work to understand how we got here in the first place so we can move forward deliberately and mindfully. As the adage implies, to move forward, it's crucial to learn from history—otherwise, we'll simply repeat it.

So let's go back for a moment to 1827. In Europe, the Greek Revolution was underway. Thousands were mourning German composer Ludwig van Beethoven in Vienna. In Egypt, the Cairo University School of Medicine was founded as the first medical school in Africa. In the United States, John Quincy Adams was the sitting president when the Baltimore and Ohio Railroad was chartered by a group of

Baltimore merchants to officially become the first North American railroad. One year later, rail transported US mail for the first time, and within several years, 2,800 miles of railway would crisscross the United States.[8]

The steam engine was revolutionary on its own, but it also spurred thousands of other innovations, including in engineering, the transportation of goods, and even tourism. While we've forgotten the impact of railroads on work, their influence was significant.

For a few hundred years, work had looked relatively the same to most people. Many families had farms or shops for traded goods. Others provided necessary services like smithing or tanning. The Industrial Revolution brought with it manufacturing environments like factories, which provided an employment outlet that was, well, revolutionary for millions. While the daily work was different across these examples, there was a similarity *about* the work: it was contained to a single environment. Everything was done in a specific place at a specific time.

Railroads changed everything. They gave people, goods, and organizations the ability to travel with more speed than ever before. They became a vital part of the economy by boosting trade and allowing merchants to quickly transport goods to new markets—railroads were the Amazon Prime of their era.

As exciting as these changes were, they also presented a unique challenge for burgeoning rail lines. They took freight and passengers across literally hundreds and thousands of miles, making multiple stops along the way at stations. Such an operation required people to not only run the individual trains but also people to oversee the trains when they stopped at each station as well as people to manage shipping and delivery to make sure the right things were unloaded in the right place at the right time. As you can imagine, there was a hiring boom.

The next time you wonder where middle managers came from, thank the railways. Deep corporate hierarchies with dozens of managers were born out of necessity. Bosses were centralized at headquarters back on the East Coast. To keep things running smoothly, though, organizations needed specialized decision-makers closer to the customer at each point in the journey. This led to station managers and regional managers that reported to corporate management. Railroads were so successful at implementing this innovative system that other industries mirrored it to expand their businesses. And the corporate hierarchy with which we've all become familiar with for the past hundred-plus years was born.

Eventually, what was once innovative, fresh, and unique became the norm. And then it not only became the norm but also the written rule of how organizations *had to be* structured. Fast-forward several generations, and even small start-ups today borrow these constructs because they are so widely accepted—and, to some degree, expected. This organizational structure is reflected in most companies operating currently, but no one asks why or where it came from.

Certainly, over the years, there have been some tweaks to the hierarchical structure introduced by the railroad industry. In the 1940s and '50s, DuPont developed and deployed *task forces* it sent out to various locations to solve specific problems. Task forces developed a reputation for agile, innovative work and solutions. A man named Wilbur "Bill" Gore worked on a DuPont task force from 1945 until 1957, which informed his ideas about how organizations should be structured. He went on to form his own company, and it has long been known as one of the best organizations to work for.

REFLECTING: THE GORE WAY

I was working for the University of Delaware in the early 1990s when the single most important event to impact my own beliefs about the workplace occurred. At the time, I was conducting research on learning environments and studying the process of how people learn skills—both in traditional learning settings and outside the classroom. While researching, I stumbled across a company called W. L. Gore & Associates, best known as the producer of Gore-Tex. A colleague of mine at the time knew of Gore because her husband worked there and told me, "They are extremely hard to get into, but those who do seem to love it."

My research into the organization uncovered many intriguing approaches at Gore. The company essentially said *no* to most of the traditional management practices seen at any other company. At the time, there were no supervisors and no job descriptions, and the only job title was "associate." Bill Gore had been so excited by his work on the smaller task forces during his time at DuPont that when he started his own company, he decided to base the company structure on the more collaborative, equitable model of task force work he'd experienced. He believed the traditional corporate hierarchy constrained people rather than generating momentum and ownership. Instead of having a "job," employees had "commitment areas." Anecdotally, when I joined the organization myself, I found that no one asked, "What's your job?" Instead, people asked, "What's your commitment?"

This difference went beyond mere semantics to the actual culture and policies of the company. During my tenure at Gore, there were four simple principles, developed by founder Bill Gore, which guided all the behaviors within the company:

1. Freedom

2. Commitment

3. Fairness

4. Waterline

This last principle was Bill Gore's way of saying that everyone was in the same boat together and should do their own part to contribute to the company's success. This emphasized a sense of ownership, responsibility, and camaraderie within the company that endures after more than half a century.

During my time at Gore, I saw how these principles played out. There was an absence of the traditional signs of organizational structure and hierarchy. For example, there were no policy manuals, and there was an absence of traditional performance reviews. Instead, associates had "contribution reviews" outlining how they had contributed to the company's success. If contributions had a tremendous impact on the business, then associates had an opportunity to receive the largest "increase." If contributions were less impactful to the organization, then the attitude was, "Hey, let's see where you're off track and how we can fix this together."

Everyone at Gore got a sponsor—not a supervisor—when they joined the company, and the role they played in an associate's success was significant but came without the traditional power of a boss. Sponsors provided influence but didn't tell associates what to do. At Gore, the focus was on maximizing "contributions," which had a specific definition: an associate's impact *times* overall effectiveness.

In short, Gore dismantled my understanding and experience of workplace culture, which to that point had been strictly hierarchical and included an unquestionable authority structure. Attracted to their approach and willingness to try something different, I wanted to work there myself. When I joined the Gore team, I pursued commitment areas in human resources as well as learning and development.

Gore is often included in lists outlining the 100 best companies to work for in the United States and abroad, and that's no accident. Today, the company has thousands of associates spread out across four continents, so they have every excuse you could imagine for "needing" the standard corporate hierarchy. Instead, they've continued Bill Gore's legacy of doing things differently, carving out their own path in the history of work.

BREAKING THE RED TAPE

The Gore way feels like a complete 180-degree turn from the railroad hierarchy, doesn't it? Mind you, I'm not saying the railroad hierarchy was wrong—it served a great purpose for its time. And it probably felt more supportive than how we think of the typical corporate structure. After all, the corporate management of the railroad was beholden to their customers, who were across the country. To prevent, mitigate, and eliminate errors in the system that could be problematic for the customer, a lot of oversight was necessary. The customer was so important that companies had to decentralize decisions from headquarters and make them closer to the customer. That approach empowered local employees, who had to be trusted to carry a lot of responsibility.

While the approach was innovative at the time, the world has continued to change. Companies continue to recycle this structure without looking for a way to be more aligned to today's needs and priorities. In his book *Creativity, Inc.*, Ed Catmull, the former president of both Pixar and Disney Animation, describes the early days of the merger between the two studios, when he was acclimating to the Disney team.

During production on the animated feature film *Bolt*, the production ran into a unique problem with a character's design. When Ed asked how long it would take to correct the problem, the team told him it would require at least six months to reconfigure the character's design, putting the production far behind schedule and way over budget.

Long story short, a few animators went rogue over the next weekend, went into the office on their own time, solved the design problem, and showed the solution to Ed the following Monday. Leadership reviewed and approved the proposed changes, meaning the production lost little time and stayed on budget.

Obviously, this disparity in the time it took to correct the problem caused Ed to do a bit of investigating. Were some team members more motivated? Faster animators? Did they see the problems differently? Turns out some of Ed's predecessors had built in so much oversight and red tape to their processes in the hope of eliminating mistakes that getting changes approved was painfully slow.

When they removed the red tape, leadership empowered animators to explore their own solutions. Animators could pitch their ideas and solutions directly to Catmull, so they sped up and improved their production process. In this approach, the Disney team provided animators with the psychological safety and creative license to be successful. As a result, *Bolt* was both a critical and commercial success, earning the studio twice what it cost to produce the film plus the animation team's first Academy Award nomination in five years.

While many organizations see their so-called competition as the enemy, their worst enemies tend to be the barriers they put in their own way. There's nothing inherently wrong with wanting to avoid mistakes. According to Catmull, Disney Animation went through a season when they were so averse to mistake making that they unintentionally limited their team's freedom, creativity, and problem-solving capabilities.[9]

Likewise, there are several examples of how the COVID-19 pandemic accelerated business plans for things like mobile orders and curbside service. Many companies had plans in the works for these services—however, because of their hierarchy, these were long-term plans because they still had to go through legal, then on to traditional operational hoops, blah, blah, blah ... you get the idea.

But then suddenly, in the early days of the pandemic, when business survival was suddenly dependent on these innovations, organizations gave themselves license to break through their own red tape at lightning speed. Long-term plans bypassed the typical corporate decision-making processes and were put into action right away. As it turns out, it worked.

> **We can be grateful for the innovations of the past without getting stuck on them. We can look back, appreciate our accomplishments, and then use that as motivation to move forward.**

Were there things that needed ironing out? Sure. But that's true of any innovation and part of the process of improvement. In the process, employees *and* customers were given the grace to refine these innovations together, understanding that it was all being worked out for the greater good.

The question is: How much more profit could have been generated if companies had instituted these innovations sooner, optimizing their systems *before* a crisis forced their hand?

In short, we can be grateful for the innovations of the past without getting stuck on them. We can look back, appreciate our accomplishments, and then use that as motivation to move forward. To tweak the words of author Marshall Goldsmith, "What got us here won't get us *there*."[10]

DRESSING FOR SUCCESS

A few years back, I heard about a situation at a major consulting firm. The company sent home the front-desk receptionist and docked her pay over a dress code violation. The issue? Management said her heels weren't high enough. She was called into a manager's office for a discussion in which the manager literally measured one of her heels. The employee asked, "Why do I have to wear two-to-four-inch heels? I'm on my feet all day, walking people to their appointments."

I'm simplifying things here, but their response was, "Because you represent the brand, and *it's the policy*."

This is a perfect example of how we often prioritize policies over people. The mandated dress code had nothing to do with the employee's success. If a person is on her feet a lot, wouldn't she be a lot more successful in her role wearing shoes that allow her to do her best work? The answer's obvious, but the company was stuck on an old view of "professional" dress code: women wear high heels; men wear suits and ties. The end.

This example is more than a violation of a policy—it is damaging to people and organizational culture, not to mention an example of gender bias. Because this book is all about a new approach to work,

I'm using the example to demonstrate how and why *better work* will also need to include *less bias and more inclusion.*

I'm not arguing that we should eliminate all dress code rules or that people should wear whatever they want at work. Far from it. After all, it'd be foolish to let someone working in a manufacturing plant to be around heavy machinery with open-toed shoes because that wouldn't be setting them up for success. Instead, it would set up a person for an injury and a company for a workers' compensation claim or possible lawsuit. No one wins in that scenario.

In other words, dressing for success is less about looks and more about whether you have the resources you need to be successful. Of course, this will look different, depending on where you are and what needs to be accomplished. We'd laugh at an Olympic figure skater wearing a hazmat suit just as much as we'd laugh at a nuclear inspector wearing ice skates. Context not only matters—but it's also essential.

I previously alluded to how, when I started with WorldatWork a few years ago, people were concerned that I'd take away casual Friday. Things are palpably different now. If you had employees working from home during the COVID-19 pandemic, do you think they wore heels, suits, or other dress code attire? Even if folks wore button-up shirts, I bet the majority wore sweatpants to round out their "work wear" since only their top half was visible during video calls. We forget the history of wearing business suits goes back several centuries to the European aristocratic tradition of attending a ruler's court. Embellished suits were worn to embody a picture of prosperity and success. Hundreds of years later, we're still stuck on that picture and reinforce formal dress codes in situations in which they add nothing to overall work performance.

Getting back to bias for a moment, we must also be mindful of policies that have nothing to do with success but everything to do with bias. This includes things like requiring that natural hair or specific styles be avoided, tattoos and piercings remain covered, or that only women wear makeup. As we face biases and stereotypes across our wider society, we must confront them in our organizational culture. Organizations and the people at their core must confront and adapt deep-seated notions of the "productive and professional" employee. Companies face disruption and possible litigation if applicants and employees suspect they were not given an opportunity or promotion because of how they look or dress. While it's possible to overdo it with policies and processes that inhibit success, there will always need to be some rules at work. Moving forward, though, we must do the hard work to ensure we aren't basing those policies on the *appearance* of success or on our own biases of what we think success should look like.

A lot of the changes we're seeing aren't really any different from other changes accelerated by previous historical events. World War II also accelerated changes in how we view work—and specifically *who* is "allowed" to work. By necessity, the war brought women into the workplace on a larger scale than ever before. The result? Good ol' Rosie the Riveter, who redefined not only the dress code for women but also showed women were capable of doing manual labor in a manufacturing environment just like their male counterparts.

The war created a broader labor pool, and I think we're seeing something similar happen today as the remote-work revolution creates new opportunities for those with location-based work requirements or who need specific accommodations at work. With more organizations open to flexible work times and locations, geographic limitations that businesses have formerly instituted are toppling quickly, which allows organizations to find the best talent available.

On that note, even the term "workplace" is outdated. While there are certainly types of work that require a specific, contained location—agriculture, for instance—the mentality of work being an actual *place* is rarely true anymore. WorldatWork's own research has shown growth in organizations that are purposefully designing full-time remote roles—rising 17 percent since 2019.[11] Remote-work solutions have been successfully applied in education, healthcare, government, law, and most service-related industries. Yet we see leaders in major banking institutions who are so focused on the historical mentality of the workplace that they've forced people back into offices—even though they could be equally successful in remote settings.

I once read a story about a business in Thailand located in an area where they have frequent, recurring flooding. This business took an innovative approach to a solution. To ensure that people could still come to work during the flood season, the business built a floating office that could rise with the water level. While I admire aspects of their ingenuity, it makes me wonder what other solutions they could have come up with if they hadn't been focused on getting people into a physical location. I mean, when and where is it so important to an organization's overall success for people to work inside a specific building during a flood? Global warming will only accelerate the number of businesses facing similar situations. Are we so convinced that work can't happen in nontraditional places, like our homes, that we have quite literally built offices to keep us working in traditional offices during natural disasters? It says a lot about where our collective focus has been for that approach to have been taken.

BRINGING YOUR FULL SELF TO WORK

More and more companies talk about how they want people to "bring their full selves" to work. To do so, organizations must figure out how to create experiences consistent with this message. Let's go back to the written and unwritten rules in organizations for a moment. While businesses have written rules about how to *be a person* at work, there are also plenty of unwritten rules about behavior and appearance at work.

Without going far back in time, until relatively recently, there was a clear line in the sand: You could be whatever and whomever you wanted *outside* the office—however, when you were at work, you had to conform your behavior to the organization's culture. Otherwise, people faced not fitting in or even getting fired. In the Old Work Exchange, you were expected to give up pieces of yourself at work to fit the mold of a "successful" employee.

While COVID-19 allowed innovations to bypass the red tape of the hierarchy, it also blurred this line in the sand. Video calls have allowed us to see into each other's homes and get to know one another on a more intimate level. The divisions between "work" and "life" collapsed as homes became "workplaces"—and people's work happened alongside schooling, healthcare, pet care, and extended-family care.

It's more important than ever that we bring our full selves to work—and that we support our teams in doing so. Buying patterns have changed, and consumer bases are more diverse than ever, so it's essential for that diversity to be reflected in our workforces. Everyone should be encouraged to contribute their thoughts and perspectives. Public messages encouraging diversity are great, but without representation and equity, we end up reverting to the same old communication patterns, meetings, decision-making, and biases. The same old stuff just isn't cutting it.

Policies in this area can help set people up for success by creating safe and equitable workplaces. However, many organizations have gotten in trouble with policies that were established for the advantage of the *employer* rather than the *employees'* success or protection. In other words, policies were for the organization instead of people, so there was a lack of alignment. Policies that are designed and enacted with an eye toward consistency haven't always led to equitable outcomes for all employees. At a minimum, they systematically prevent individuals from being themselves at work.

Gender and racial pay gaps are obvious examples, but there are also issues that pop up at companies that aren't so obvious: pay differences based on personal attributes, access to leadership for sharing ideas or mentoring, and the ability to engage in highly visible projects. In many ways, these issues can propel or sink careers.

> **It's imperative that we regularly audit our policies by asking: "Has this been designed to enable people to do their absolute best work?"**

Encouraging people to bring their full selves to work requires a balance with policies, which must be fair and provide freedom to individuals, but also collectively fair so *everyone* can succeed. And that's where we must go back to our core concept about policies: above all else, policies must set people up for success. It's imperative that we regularly audit our policies by asking: "Has this been designed to enable people to do their absolute best work?"

If the answer is "No," then tweak and shift things until you can say "Yes." This isn't a onetime question. It's something to check in on regularly. Our answers directly impact the bottom line. How we treat people at work influences how we treat customers.

MAKING CURRENCY SHIFTS

The pandemic revealed how work culture was vulnerable and where we'd gotten too complacent doing things in historical ways. It also has shown us where *human capital* (people) can be replaced with *automated capital* (machines, not people). We've got robots delivering pizzas to people and drones dropping life preservers in the oceans for swimmers in trouble—something unthinkable a few years ago. It's very telling that you can get a robot-delivered manicure now. Rather than seeing developments like this as a threat, we need to find ways to redistribute ourselves across organizations to create value.

Don't wait for your organization to do this *for you*—again, people are at the core of an organization! But human performance will soon be the result of human-machine partnership, which will require a new level of collaboration and interdependence with technology. If you think this is too future oriented, try living a day without your most trusted companion: your phone.

This isn't exactly a new concept either. Any time an advancement in technology has caused a major disruption to an industry, we've reallocated and retrained ourselves. When people stopped riding horses everywhere, society didn't need blacksmiths as much. But you know what we did need? Tire shops.

Another way to look at it is this: it's not the product that matters, but the people. Do we—do our people—have the skills, resources, and tools that we need for our best work? With the speed of life and work, the future isn't a bad place to start investing your resources—after all, it's where we're all headed, whether we like it or not.

At this point, you might be asking, "Scott, I'm struggling to do *my* best at work because it has changed so much. Now you are saying

I have to think about robots? So how do I motivate myself, and how do we motivate one another in this new approach to work?"

In the Old Work Exchange, there was mostly one type of currency—cold, hard cash. With the first Industrial Revolution, there was a hiring boom. Companies had absolute control over what employees made—no ifs, ands, or buts. Too often, the attitude was, "If you don't like the pay or work conditions, then you don't have to work here." People were seen as part of the machine, replaceable parts, so there was no incentive for the business to pay more or make efforts toward treating people in the ways they wanted, needed, and deserved.

Eventually, labor unions came along to speak up for workers' rights. For decades, unions have played a significant role in the safety, health, and wellness of workers. However, the reasons unions exist are absolutely part of the *Old* Work Exchange, and I'm disappointed to see that some organizations are *still* unable—or unwilling—to adapt to the current needs of people without unionization. It speaks volumes about the lack of alignment between organizations and people. Lots of books have covered the many labor strikes and movements that helped generate not only better wages but also another form of currency—better working conditions—so we won't go into detail here.

The important facet to understand: This *isn't* the first currency shift the modern world has experienced. Movements related to wages paved the way for changes in work hours and working conditions, which in turn paved the way for the next currency shift, which related to employee benefits.

In 1946, the US government tried to rein in inflation by freezing compensation, which limited companies in how much they could pay workers.[12] To attract top talent, organizations got creative, so benefits became the other big bucket to play with, and they started coming up with nonmonetary perks: job titles, health insurance, retirement accounts. Since these forms of compensation weren't taxed, it ended up being a win-win for both companies and workers as a new form of currency within the work exchange of that era.

In the New Work Exchange, currency priorities continue to shift quickly. At the core of the changes are organizations aligning with people's needs. To attract and retain people, lots of companies are struggling to catch up to meet demands. We've got fast-food chains offering free iPhones[13] to new hires and trying out daily pay.[14] Many companies are posting their benefits on their websites and adding new ones, such as mental-health resources, adoption assistance, or even unlimited paid time off. Acquiring the best talent is no longer just about salary— rather, *talent acquisition and retention are based on an organization's alignment to a candidate's needs and values.*

> **Talent acquisition and retention are based on an organization's alignment to a candidate's needs and values.**

A currency shift has occurred, and it's detectable in the questions candidates are asking in interviews. Questions are precursors for people's expectations of the workplace. Here are a few queries that prospective team members are now asking:

- Will the company allow me to work remotely or allow a hybrid schedule?

- How are the company's policies and practices combating climate change?

- Can I bring my pet to work with me?

- Has the CEO issued a statement about racial or social justice in the past several years?

- What is the organization's position on pay transparency?

- How is the organization addressing racial- and gender-based pay gaps?

- How diverse are members of the senior management and the board?

- Does the benefits package include supplementary provisions for mental-health services that put treatment in real reach without creating stigma?

- What diversity, inclusion, belonging, and antiracism programs exist within the company?

These are the kinds of questions that would've been taboo even just a few years ago. There's been a shift in mindset from just "Tell me about the job" to "How is this company going to treat me as a person?" Candidates *and* current employees are making decisions about where they want to work based not only on salary and benefits but on value alignment. There's a higher level of intimacy, authenticity, and transparency in the interview process than ever before.

If you're a people manager in any capacity, whether in HR, C-suite leadership, or even middle management, if you haven't run into such questions, then you're about to. Figuring out how to answer these questions is only one piece of the equation. The bigger issue is figuring out what your organization *values* and how that aligns with everything from your mission statement to your HR policies, from your benefits package to your internal messaging and everything in between. People's priorities span work-life balance, wellness, health, and financial stability as well as diversity, equity, and inclusion (DEI)—among other things.

In a 2021 WorldatWork study, 34 percent of prospective employees reported that a company's DEI priorities were extremely influential in their job decisions, which indicates that we're missing out on more than one-third of available talent if it's not an organizational priority.[15] While the list of priorities included here looks substantial, it's not exhaustive. Organizations need a holistic, comprehensive strategy for aligning to and providing for people's needs at work—also known as a Total Rewards strategy.

To that end, organizations should prepare to break down barriers that haven't been addressed. A popular meme recounts how employees with families are often expected to work like they don't have kids and parent like they don't have a job. How can we, as colleagues and influencers in organizations, address this discrepancy?

GETTING PRACTICAL

Work always has and will move in a forward direction. Are we moving with it or not? Are you on board or on the sidelines as the New Work Exchange is developed without you? A lot of the discussion so far in this chapter has focused on the historical and the philosophical, so I want to make sure we also explore the practical. Let's look at the things we *can* control so that none of us are left behind.

> Are you on board or on the sidelines as the New Work Exchange is developed without you?

Some of the tips we're about to cover relate to both organizations and people within them—others apply more directly to individuals within organizations who have roles that influence or design roles. However, there are key messages in each tip that apply to anyone who works.

THINKING CREATIVELY GOES A LONG WAY

Trying things for the first time or finding a new way to do things is full of creativity. Have the recent changes in daily work life made you see ways to bring a little creative thinking to your role, team, or organization? Are the changes based on technology, strategy, or process, or are they people focused? How do they benefit your organization's bottom line?

For example, there are companies that have let their employees go fully remote, allowing them to move from high-cost areas like San Francisco and relocate to areas where they can afford to buy homes for less than they were renting. Such a move can create many positive effects: it might improve an employee's quality of life, support the trust and loyalty people feel toward a company, and increase productivity as the employee becomes less stressed about money or feels closer to family.

In a purely organizational example, a creative solution for capacity is to leverage new technology to increase workflow. To increase the number of hours devoted to projects, it's possible to hire global vendor teams that continue working on projects after a company's main offices are closed. Time zones of productivity can be added without having to create a second-and third-shift system of work in an organization's home country, increasing capacity on projects and generating more revenue.

What innovations, efficiencies, or new streams of revenue are hiding in plain sight? Are you creating the means for those ideas to be shared and assessed?

In the same book I mentioned before, *Creativity, Inc.*, Catmull shares how they created something called Notes Day at Pixar. Literally any employee—from environmental services to the art department, from marketing to accounting, from finance to HR—could submit notes on how to improve the company. They had a process for consolidating the notes, creating diverse task forces representing every department of the company, and putting together action plans on the notes that could have the greatest immediate impact.

IDENTIFYING AND IMPROVING SKILLS DEFICITS

As companies quickly adjusted to lockdown restrictions during the pandemic—getting Zoom accounts, installing messenger tools—these disruptions showed there was a deficit in technical and digital skills among the workforce. Many people struggled to use these tools—even getting computers set up correctly at home without in-person IT support stumped many people. Again, while these examples seem like challenges, they're also opportunities. The worst thing we can do on this side of the pandemic is say, "Well, I'm glad we

Individually and organizationally, we have obvious areas for ongoing development. Let's figure out what they are and address them.

finally got through *that* mess," and not apply the lessons learned. Individually and organizationally, we have obvious areas for ongoing development. Let's figure out what they are and address them.

Once we've identified areas in which we're skill deficient, we can work to catch up on these skills. For example, we can design and implement short, easy trainings for people to improve their digital fluency. What aspects of onboarding and staff development did we adjust during the pandemic? Can we make them permanent aspects of our processes? There's no shortage of tools available to companies to conduct skills training in digital environments. We all love a good "lunch and learn," so what's stopping you from using a delivery service to get the team a meal and allowing people to complete training at a time best suited to their schedule?

Alongside the human element of this, we also need to ask, "Where are our systems still deficit?" I encountered a situation in which a woman was trying to use her paid time off (PTO). She literally had her phone in her hand, ready to book a flight and an Airbnb in France—which she could do instantaneously. Unfortunately, due to a lag in the system, her HR department couldn't tell her what her PTO balance was. The number of approvals and system updates it took to get the information prevented on-demand and immediate action. Instead, it took forty-eight hours and an email to her supervisor before she knew her PTO balance and could book her trip. Hope she was still able to get her reservations.

In this digital age, there's no room or excuse for a deficit in technology—not when it comes to remaining competitive and not when it comes to taking care of people. These are all fixable issues that show where organizations truly place their value.

I know the bottom-line-inclined professionals out there, often accountable to COOs and CFOs, just see dollar signs when I say all this, but what's more expensive over the long term? Investing in some new tools and methods to develop your team and close the skills gaps? Or galvanizing the status quo, losing people to other companies, and having to pay the turnover costs? Not to mention the costs for the loss of skills and experience. Either way, there's a cost, and yes, we must pick an approach.

REVISITING YOUR ROLES, TITLES, AND JOB DESCRIPTIONS

There have been so many shifts at work in the past several years that people often feel they are wearing *way too many hats*. Many people have changed roles, and many organizations have created new jobs very quickly. With all the change, are they the right roles, titles, and descriptions? People, managers, and HR can come together to have some productive, intersectional discussions—and the spark for the conversations can come from any direction.

If you see a lack of alignment in your role or job description, have a proactive conversation with a leader. Come prepared with solutions, options, and possible changes. As a manager or HR partner, you can have an immediate impact in attracting and retaining talent by addressing potential issues that you see. Are you hiring for jobs that need to be done today or the skills your organization will need long term? Are there people on teams who could thrive if roles were adjusted? Do job descriptions or titles need to be reconsidered? Adjust to new trends by adapting how you approach and write job descriptions. Continue to include the necessary qualifications and skills, as long as they're written in the context of what will make people successful in roles.

If you are looking to fill a role, is it time to be increasingly flexible and open about the skills and background a person needs for the role? For example, college degrees are becoming less relevant for many roles. They don't necessarily predict a person's ability to be successful. Were important skills developed without earning a formal degree?

We also tend to put as much into a job description as possible. Are the listed requirements too lofty or unrealistic for the role? Consider alternatives, including certifications or ongoing training *after* hiring. In general, we should hire for where we want people to be *going*, not for where they *are*. In an ongoing period of change, we don't just want more of the same. We want people who are cultural adds—contributors to an organization's culture—while they are performing essential tasks, so design and adjust roles accordingly.

This includes writing job descriptions to define the kind of people we're looking for in roles instead of just standard skills and experience. Be deliberate about what a role truly needs. Is it someone who'll follow an established process and not ask questions? Or is it someone innovative and experimental? Is there a profile of success in your organization? Do you want more of that or a different flavor? Most job descriptions don't mention speed, but it is a great skill to prioritize in recruitment.

In other words, design your roles and job descriptions to be about more than the job. Make them about the organization itself. What's your organizational purpose, what's your mission, and how do you make an impact in the world? Do your roles and job descriptions align with what you've described? Why should people work for you? What are your organizational values, and are you embedding them in your descriptions to ensure alignment with people? The roles for which we hire give people an opportunity to opt in or out based on what we sort, signal, and organize conceptually into our descriptions.

Writing job descriptions with the New Work Exchange's mindset is challenging at first, but it helps us attract the best candidates—those with the right skill sets and aligned values. Going forward, job descriptions must reflect essential functions *as well as* be pithy, cogent, and include a vision of potential for the role.

ESTABLISHING FORWARD MOTION

It's easy to feel exhausted from all that's changed recently. Historical events and technological changes have always played major roles in changing our perspectives on work. Looking back, we see that the Old Work Exchange was a long-term agreement between the employer and employee that really amounted to a transactional relationship. As an employee gained experience and gained tenure at an organization, their compensation would reflect this. That was the extent of the exchange.

This approach is no longer enough for people—if it ever really was at all! We need to accept that it's time for work to evolve because people have evolved.

People rarely stay at jobs for twenty or thirty years, and the best talent can't simply be bought for a price. If we're honest with ourselves, don't most of us want to have our organizations recognize that we are worth more than a paycheck? We all want to make a difference in the world and feel valued as individuals.

Workplaces are becoming more honest and transparent—mostly because employees and candidates are demanding high levels of honesty and transparency. The companies that resist and hold on stubbornly to the Old Work Exchange will eventually figure out it's not because of a labor shortage—it's because no one wants the currency they're offering. But by the time they figure it out, it'll be too late.

So it's time to get honest and move forward. How do *you* define work? How does your organization define it? How are changes in technology and culture making you reassess your perspective of work? What elements of the Old Work Exchange are still reflected in your organization? Which ones need to be replaced or retired?

Seriously, take some time to think it over. Otherwise, what's the point? Now that we've had a chance to examine where our notions of work originated, let's look at what we can leave in the past so we don't hold onto the wrong things as we embrace the New Work Exchange.

CHAPTER 3

Walking Away from Obsolete Practices

I n the last chapter, we talked about the historical background for many of our workplace practices and beliefs. What we've begun to unravel is that the new practices, structures, mindsets, and methodologies we need at work come with some hard truths: work doesn't really suck. Neither does Monday. What does? All the baggage we have about work!

We hold on to the idea that we *have to* do specific things to be effective, but many of those approaches were established for the Old Work Exchange. When we continue relying on outdated, obsolete concepts at work, it weighs us down. But if we can leave the baggage behind, *work starts to get better.*

Across this chapter, we'll look at examples of obsolete practices we need to leave behind. We'll also analyze why many organizations are struggling to abandon the things we all know aren't working but choose to settle for instead. We've gotten stuck, and the cause of our paralysis is more than just change being difficult. We must address what's commonly called the *adaptability paradox* and how it creeps into work.

Then we'll look at a common attribute in companies that are holding onto obsolete practices: remaining too centralized in their structure for effective (and fast) decision-making. While practices, processes, and policies can be guiding forces, adherence to any extreme usually blinds us from seeing reality.

For example, there was once an incident in an outlet of a famous restaurant chain when the host refused to seat a guest because her entire party hadn't yet arrived. The woman asked several times to be seated, even going so far as to say she'd order for her family before they arrived. The host refused, stating it was "against policy." She was dehydrated, and when the woman stood up, she fell and hit her head.

When culture or policy blinds us from what is quite literally standing in front of us, then it's time to make a move. We need to be asking, "Are we people first, or are we putting policy, history, time, tradition, or what's worked previously *first?*"

Work is an emotional construct. It's always personal, and that includes when we're doing business as a customer. In any scenario—employee or customer—when policies, hierarchies, processes, or profits are prioritized over people, there's an inherent risk lurking in the business. That's doubly true if the situation is related to obsolete methods of working. If we refuse to change what we know is outdated, that's neglectful.

Moving on from obsolete versions of work requires that we pause and ask some very direct questions about work, including, "Do we really care about people here?" When we empower and humanize the individuals we've hired for their skills, ability, and knowledge, we end up discovering obstacles that do way more damage than good.

REFLECTING: TOUGH BUSINESS IS BAD BUSINESS

In a previous role, I found myself in an awkward position. I was working in the company's global talent division, where I ran several functions—one of them being recruiting. There were written and unwritten rules that dictated who could "interview" candidates. One rule prevented less-senior employees from actively conducting interviews with senior candidates. That is, if the job's title put a candidate "higher on the food chain," then team members weren't allowed to conduct formal interviews. It was fine to "meet and greet" candidates in such scenarios, but the meeting wasn't a "formal interview," and traditional "interview-type questions" were forbidden. My heavy use of quotation marks here should convey how much red tape and nuance there was with this approach.

My title was such that this rule rarely posed a problem. However, when I found myself in a room alongside a junior recruiter who was part of my team, meeting with a candidate for an executive vice president position, the problems with this title-centric fixation were brought into vivid focus.

Whomever filled this role was going to be my boss, so I was very interested in the outcome. The recruitment team set up a "noninterview" for the junior recruiter and me, during which we were expected to have a conversation with the candidate about her experience and get to know her personality. We'd then share our observations with the CEO, who'd make the final hiring decision.

Just to underscore that my meeting was a noninterview, the CEO came down to my office before my meeting and said, "I just want to remind you, this is *not* an interview."

While many thoughts flew through my head at that precise moment, what flew out of my mouth was compliance. "Sure," I said. "I get it."

Seconds later, I had also updated my social media that I was "open to discussing jobs."

Part of the problem with this noninterview was that the candidate—we'll call her Donna—knew she was meeting with two people who'd report to her. Interacting with potential new bosses can absolutely be a good thing. It provides valuable insight into how candidates treat people who are "lower" on the corporate ladder.

In fact, I've seen organizations ask receptionists how candidates treated them during check-in: "Were they condescending? Were they demanding? Rude? Impatient?" Candidates go into an interview room ready to impress whomever is there. Covert feedback can be a way to weed out the wrong candidates. Interactions with people whom candidates *don't* have to impress is an incredibly important gauge for their potential success.

During the lunch, the junior recruiter asked Donna a question that veered a bit toward the personal. It was something like, "What do you like to do in your free time?" Just a common *get-to-know-you* question, which technically was part of the purpose of this noninterview.

Now Donna could have responded in many ways. She could've shared a couple of hobbies. Or if she didn't feel comfortable discussing any aspect of her personal life, she could've easily diverted or made a lighthearted joke like, "Well, I'm afraid if I start listing them off, then you'll realize how weird I actually am and not want to continue talking with me." Any of these responses would've been fine and appropriate.

Instead, Donna's quip back to the junior recruiter was, "I think that's a little above your pay grade."

The effect was immediate. It shut down the conversation, and the junior recruiter was put in check. It immediately changed the dynamic between Donna and me because it confirmed to me she wasn't the right person to lead the team.

But it wasn't my decision. Technically, it wasn't even an interview. In such a title-centric culture, I played my part in a title-centric conversation during which the candidate gave a title-centric response. I gave my feedback—including my concerns about the interaction with the junior associate. Ultimately, Donna was hired. My junior recruiter resigned, and one month later, I moved on too.

In theory, title-centric cultures signal how important *some* people are. The downside is this creates a robust sense of *unimportance* for many others.

Let me pause for a second here and clarify something: organizations can have titles that create rank and hierarchy and still have healthy cultures. Some organizations equate titles with importance instead of what they truly are—merely descriptions of the work people are doing. Titles signal the essentials of a role, but within some organizations, they reflect an assumed level of importance that isn't earned or legitimate.

Operating and reinforcing a title-centric culture means we often end up hiring the *role*, not the *person,* which often leads to massive business implications. A symptom of such a cultural approach can often be seen when a team starts to underperform. Roles are often created for a hire to come in and *fix* things. Frequently, it ends up being a person who will play "hardball."

That was the case here—the organization wanted a candidate to play hardball and be tough. The executive team thought the interaction between Donna and the junior recruiter was *tough* business when really it was *bad* business. Caught up in trying to fix things, the executive team neglected to ask one fundamental question: "What type of person would truly enable the team to do their best work?"

Hiring someone to fix teams only works when you want the existing team to leave. Whom we hire and whom we reward are two of the most influential and impactful elements of overall organizational performance. If we don't focus on hiring practices that support our best work, we're focused on enabling outdated work.

Ironically, I'd been hired to help that company evolve from their very hierarchical organizational and command structure to a culture where "everyone counted." The problem wasn't the statement— everyone *should* count—but the lack of conviction to make it happen. Too many executive teams get caught up in what they think *sounds* or *looks* good, like being "a great place to work," but when it comes time to make it happen, they don't want to do the required work. Everyday work has to be about more than optics. Yes, "if you build it, they will come," but if you say it and *don't* build it, they'll most certainly leave.

It's more damaging to say you want everyone to count and then do nothing to make it happen. In case you are wondering what happened to Donna, she left within the year.

WORKING WITH THE ADAPTABILITY PARADOX

One of the most popularly quoted definitions of insanity is "doing the same thing over and over again and expecting different results." While many people attribute the quote to Einstein, one of its first appearances in print was in an Alcoholics Anonymous pamphlet from the 1980s.[16] Chances are, you've heard this phrase and nodded along in agreement—or you've even said it to others. But if we take a moment to be introspective, we can likely recall moments where we've done the same thing repeatedly, expecting different results without a modicum of improvement.

This is what's known as the *adaptability paradox*—the tendency to default to a comfortable practice, even when we know the practice isn't in our best interest. The expression has been around a long time, but a 2021 McKinsey article explains that this tendency occurs "when we most need to learn and change, [but] we stick with what we know, often in a way that stifles learning and innovation."[17] Many organizations hold on to what they know they're comfortable with—even when they know it's not working well or leads to resignations. Did the company I worked for adapt its approach after Donna left? I wasn't there anymore, but through former colleagues, I learned the answer was a resounding *no*.

> **If adaptation is crucial for businesses to thrive and survive, then why do we resist adaptation?**

If adaptation is crucial for businesses to thrive and survive, then why do we resist adaptation? We often prioritize hiring people who are adaptable. We look for team members who have experienced different working conditions and situations as well as demonstrated the ability to learn, relearn, and apply skills across different scenarios. But we still cling tightly to the status quo when we know our organizations benefit from new ideas and solutions.

Part of this is just instinct. When our brains encounter something new or challenging, or we find ourselves in trouble, our instinctive response is to find comfort. We fall back on behaviors or activities that soothe us, which are usually something we *know* or *have done*. However, those moments on the brink, full of new decisions so crucial for improvement and progress, are exactly when we need to leave the past behind.

Developing what's known as "muscle memory" for new things requires that we fight the instinct to repeat the past. The brain is a large muscle. We only develop new neural pathways and rewire the brain when we repeatedly *follow through with new things.* Adoption of a practice demands we try things and repeat them.

The adaptability paradox is a major obstacle in business. Rewiring an entire corporation's "brain" is a monumental task, and it's pointless to pretend otherwise. It's so monumental that many leaders just won't tackle it—it's too difficult to execute and too much of a disruption from what's comfortable, even if comfort means eventual extinction.

Awareness is the first step to change. When we become aware of the adaptability paradox, it doesn't facilitate change but equips us to recognize what we're fighting against. Embracing a new era of work is a bit like training for a marathon. The first stages involve a lot of discomfort. We need to lean into discomfort, and while awareness doesn't alleviate the pain, it sets proper expectations, which helps us adapt to changes.

While they've become cliché examples, Blockbuster Video and Kodak are great examples of companies falling prey to the adaptability paradox. That's exactly *why* they've become clichés, after all—they weren't willing to change their approach or business as the world around them changed. They clung to their business model, which had once led to their growth, unable to break from the comfort zone in which they were trapped.

What made us successful yesterday won't guarantee success tomorrow. Athletes tweak their training to make improvements. Chefs adjust recipes to improve the full experience of a dish. Sometimes edits and small changes aren't enough. To overcome the adaptability paradox and bring work into a new age, we must first admit that the paradox affects us all. Then, it's time to overhaul practices and make bold changes. The next step we'll take in ushering in a new era of contemporary work may feel like a drastic change for many.

DECENTRALIZING DECISIONS AND EMPOWERING NEW CONTROLS

One of the greatest outcomes of the pandemic was the forced decentralization of work. Under stress, many companies discovered they were too centralized, slow, and unresponsive to meet the needs of their stakeholders, employees, and customers. While some companies have learned from the experience and decentralized to improve their response times, others stuck to outdated policies that promote compliance and complacency. The latter companies blame the crisis *for* their problems instead of recognizing the crisis merely *exposed* the problems that were already there.

Let's return to my story about Donna for a moment to give some context to what decentralizing can look like. As I mentioned, titles aren't a bad thing. Sometimes, titles are even required by articles of incorporation. They can be helpful for communication, compensation practices, fairness, and consistency. However, when titles guide most aspects of your culture, including who can interview candidates, problems arise. The company's title-centric approach was symptomatic of a bigger issue—centralized decision-making, which often signals a lack of trust.

The rule that prevented me from interviewing Donna, who was recruited for a role hierarchically above mine, meant my feedback didn't count, which meant I didn't count. While I wanted to rise above it as a professional, the experience impacted me on a personal level.

Deep down, I felt invited to stop caring about the organization and my role—so I started planning my exit. When we enable hierarchy within our organizations, we take power and agency away from the people closest to a situation, and we rob our best people of the chance to handle tasks. Problems should be solved by those who can improve the quality of the decision, even if their titles imply otherwise.

In that scenario, I was the closest to our recruitment constraints and the needs of the team. Had the decision-making process been decentralized or more inclusive, then we could have collectively addressed the team's gaps. Instead, we created additional problems, which included the team's eventual mass exodus.

Maybe you're thinking, "Scott, sounds to me like you're just angry they hired someone you didn't like." But for me, this was more about a missed opportunity. In the long run, I'm thankful because, regardless of who was hired, it showed me I didn't want to *be there* any longer. If anything, it just expedited finding my next opportunity and provided clarity on what helped me do my best work.

Let's go back to the historical relevance of the railroad industry for a moment. There were middle managers galore. Railroad leadership was centralized back at the "home office" on the East Coast, but those localized managers were empowered to make decentralized decisions. As other industries adopted railroad-style hierarchy, we seem to have lost touch with the balance of centralized and decentralized decisions the railroad's framework facilitated. Instead, we kept the wide and deep railroad hierarchy—with decisions and control being centralized.

The impact of this approach is still recognizable in our businesses today. Are we in the same world? No, we aren't. We live in a far more connected, consumer-facing world than in the railroad baron era, so decision-making needs to be further decentralized and moved to the person who's closest to the customer or issue at hand.

When making decisions about internal issues, executive teams are likely not aware of daily operational issues because their primary focus is usually external. If we want to know what's really happening inside our organizations, we should talk to those who are *in it* every day—they have a better and more accurate perspective, which can be incredibly valuable for businesses.

Philosophically, most people tend to agree with this. We don't want the CEO fixing the salesperson's computer—we want them focused on leading the business to its future destination. When companies had to convert to a work-from-home approach during the COVID-19 pandemic, many were surprised they could still get the same output—sometimes more—without having people in the office. The perception was that supervisors needed to hover over people for focus and output. Companies had to trust employees more with decision-making processes, like when they'd get to their desk, take their lunch, and close up for the day. Up to that point, such activities had been managed and enforced through hierarchical employee structure as well as cultural norms and behavior signals within the physical structure of the workplace.

WorldatWork's research shows there's been continued growth for organizations that design full-time remote roles, with an increase of 72 percent productivity in 2021 compared to 55 percent in 2019.[18] While not every business or role can go fully remote, it demonstrates that decentralizing aspects of work yields more output than micromanagement.

Within physical workplaces, many workers stay at their desks until bosses leave just to give the appearance of productivity. Rather than working, they do nonproductive activities to fill the time. When we're paying people for their time and not their outcomes, it speaks volumes about how we're approaching our business. It's *always* more valuable to pay people for outcomes, and most companies are overdue in making this important shift. Leaders don't go to shareholder meetings with a graphic demonstrating total hours worked by salaried employees—they show outcomes. We need to be reflecting this approach in how we design roles, work, and workplaces. In a work-from-home setting, perceived pressure is lessened, which gives people more time to get things done.

In general, it's time to retire the Monday-through-Friday, nine-to-five mentality of working. Both the song and the movie are great—decades later, they retain their significance *because* we should be well beyond the limitations of nine to five at this point. But sadly, we're *not*. Dolly Parton's song, originally released in 1980 on an album titled *9 to 5 and Odd Jobs*, has such enduring relevance that in 2022, Parton released a new version of the song with Kelly Clarkson. We're on our way to a *New* Work Exchange, and we're still contending with and trying to solve issues characteristic of the *Old* Work Exchange. I'd argue that's why the song and movie remain so beloved and relevant.

People want and need to fit both work *and* their lives into twenty-four hours. That means playing with their kids when they get home from school, meeting up with a friend who needs encouragement, as well as balancing some regular "me" time and self-care. Yes, that might mean they are doing a bit of work at night after the kids are in bed or responding to an email ping after hours. That's a by-product of being empowered to decide *when* to get things done.

We aren't all at our best between nine and five, and the most successful outcomes can be correlated with people determining *where* and *how* to be the most productive. The adage "Work smarter, not harder" is partially right. I'd add that we should work when we're at our smartest, which for me is early mornings. Our goal should be the quickest and most direct path to the outcomes we're seeking, not the one that produces more or unnecessary work.

While many of us have already taken some steps toward decentralization—for example, by having teams work remotely—it's imperative to determine whether there's been a shift in overall mindset. Has the practice of decentralization really been adopted? Is new cultural muscle memory being developed, or are we reverting to old habits while we're using modern monitors?

> **It's imperative to determine whether there's been a shift in overall mindset.**

We're past due in empowering people to work toward their outcomes. Instead, we remain rooted in the mindset of needing to show "on" status, as if work is measured by the construct of time. That's still the nine-to-five, Monday-through-Friday mindset—not the mindset of someone wanting to tap the fuller potential of their people.

It's important for all leaders in organizations to grapple with a burning question: If someone only works five hours today, do you feel like the organization has been cheated? If a person is paid for eight hours of work but finishes early and decides to take in a movie, then what's your instinctive response? This is an important distinction for leaders who want the absolute best from people but still insist on their "butts in seats" mentality. We've grown accustomed to thinking such an approach delivers outcomes, but the kind of innovative, exceptional outcomes we need are delivered by people with lives that will vary from day to day. A person who feels chained to a desk is likely not engaged at work.

So when things like this happen in your organization, how do you respond? Let's flip the script again: As a person at work—wherever that work happens—do you feel tethered to a seat within specific hours? What led to that conditioning, and are you ready to let go of it? Can you help influence a different mindset within your organization?

Working at Gore made such an impression on me. They weren't just ahead of their time or prescient—their approach to work was logical, productive, and outcome based. Everything was cultivated to support people's contributions. If contributions (another term for outcomes) weren't where they needed to be, then we asked what adjustments needed to be made for change. Instead, many workplaces are still writing people up for being late or wearing too low of a heel, which only destroys productivity and trust.

Instead, set guidelines, give people a bit of choice, and hold them accountable for the important stuff, like the missed goal or the team output that was impacted.

There's no doubt that rigid work schedules are becoming obsolete, especially given the fact that 2021 was the most profitable year for companies on record since 1950.[19] Yet once state-mandated COVID-19 restrictions were lifted, we saw a host of companies trying to rush people back into the workplace.

But why? Should we care where people work if companies have been productive and profitable?

That's a trick question, because yes, we *should* care. We should be drilling into the effects of work from home—but not so much about a lack of worker productivity. We need to understand how to positively influence connectivity and collaboration without a central hub like an office bringing people together. A greater number of employees will consider relocating because of their technical ability to work from anywhere.

People are ready to establish new paths, habits, and processes. Are employers? Are organizations reluctant to solidify remote work because it requires that we stop focusing on the number of hours worked and develop a new way of measuring output? Well, that change was already overdue, and I don't foresee it going back. Thus, let's focus on ensuring that this era—characterized by a new work exchange—is a true collaboration between employer and employee. Alignment is overdue.

Every company likes to say its people are its greatest asset. Optics are powerful forces, but optics aren't enough. Far fewer companies have gone through the rigor of *showing* people that they are an organization's most valuable asset.

Let me ask you some questions: Was your team hired to work or be told what to do? Were team members hired for their skills, abilities, and insights? If so, let's leverage the brainpower that's at the core of your team to create solutions and outcomes that benefit your organization. There's great power in giving a team the chance to chime in on decisions impacting them. If people are your greatest asset, then give them the opportunity to prove it when they are working *in* and *on* the business.

> **Let's focus on ensuring that this era—characterized by a new work exchange—is a true collaboration between employer and employee. Alignment is overdue.**

Decentralizing decision-making in organizations has challenges but is one of the best ways to engage people. It unearths disagreements in perspective—for example, employees and managers who don't agree on a process, strategy, or approach. But in discomfort also lies opportunity.

When we take an intentional look at the decision-making practices happening in our organizations, we reveal patterns showing how and where decision-making occurs. Decentralizing doesn't mean leadership has no influence on process—it just means that outdated policies and people too far from decisions may not be in the best position to make a call. We need to push out some decisions to rest with our people and see how it helps invite people into our organizations in a different, more meaningful way. When people are allowed to own the outcome as part of their daily work, it redefines work. A job is doing what we are told—work is using our skills and insights.

Making decisions for a business creates a fundamentally different work experience. Going back to the example about the woman trying to be seated at the restaurant, we should enable employees to make good decisions, not just to follow a prescription without exceptions. There are always exceptions in life. Empowered team members embrace decentralized practices, and the effect soon reaches beyond customer interactions, where they are critically important. When a team is entrusted with decisions, the impact begins to ripple out into hiring practices, performance reviews, communication, collaboration, and overall creativity too!

The lack of control people experience in the workplace has long been a reason that many have felt even resentful toward leadership and work in general. Lack of control leads to a lack of alignment, which is when work becomes a job.

Think about it: when the nationwide rail strike almost happened in 2022, it was largely due to their attendance policy! The engineers and conductors were tired of being written up for taking time off. To quote one article about the threatened strike: "They're tired of unpredictable, inflexible work schedules. They're tired of being penalized for taking days off when they're sick or tending to a family emergency. They want a better quality of life."[20]

Does that quote apply to you, your team, and your organization? I'm sure it does because it's a *universal need*. While some companies aren't eager to give up control, others are waking up to the fact that putting control into the hands of employees creates a more satisfied, engaged, and productive team that produces better results—which, in the end, is good for businesses.

Organizations have a choice: they can try to hold on to the heavy-handed control of yesterday and deal with a revolving door of employees, *or* they can give folks greater influence and control over their day-to-day lives. Empowering people doesn't mean there are no rules or different rules for different people. It just means people know where they stand and what level of control they have over their own lives. People don't like "gray spaces" of uncertainty—we thrive when there's certainty and clarity. For people to commit to an organization's goals and success, uncertainty must be minimized and influence maximized.

I'm not advocating anarchy at work, nor am I suggesting that organizations abandon their titles or structures. There are just *different* and *new* ways to get great work done. What we've discovered in the postpandemic workplace is that the need for speed, flexibility, self-care, and agility we encountered *en masse* generated a new expectation for work and how consumers spend. We have opportunities to involve our teams in better, smarter, and bolder ways. We've opened the door to greater efficiency, innovation, and trust. Why would we close that door now? The New Work Exchange awaits us on the door's other side. Let's intentionally cross the threshold together.

PROVOKING CULTURAL TURNOVER

Decentralization is another way of saying "Stop micromanaging everything." When we decentralize, control shifts and rebalances. People have more work options than ever before. With those options, they want more involvement in how, where, when, and why they work. The uptick in US union activity and interest isn't without merit—it's the result of outdated management practices that no longer fit the modern-day employee.

Cultural change within our organizations is a by-product of decentralization, but it's also something we should cultivate. Companies can fall back on the adaptability paradox and say they're more comfortable with how things worked in the past, which will lead to a further breakdown of trust. Or organizations can enable a cultural reset that'll help them attract and retain the right people. There's a strong likelihood you'll have to thoughtfully provoke cultural change within your organization—it won't happen by chance.

Culture isn't just social events that help colleagues bond or regular traditions within an organization. Culture is about how and why we work. An organization's mission and goals are critical to culture. Take Movement Mortgage, based in Charlotte, North Carolina. Their website doesn't have the typical mortgage industry language guaranteeing "the best rate" or a "quick and easy loan process." Instead, they lead with mission and culture: "Movement does things differently. Building schools. Uplifting communities. Oh, and redefining the mortgage process, too." Their business output—mortgages—is presented almost as an afterthought.

Their website goes on to claim, "We give away our profits. Yes, really. With no Wall Street investors to repay, almost half of our profits go to Movement Foundation to help uplift our communities."[21] They make it clear their goal is to create opportunity across communities. Mortgages aren't the company's driving purpose—rather, mortgages enable their driving purpose.

While profit is still an essential goal for any organization, there's a growing, emerging movement toward work being a fundamental way to make a difference. Embracing that cultural shift starts with a change in mindset. It's vital to consider where we can pivot from saying, "We produce X service or product" to "We make the world a better place as a result of X service or product." In other words, "Hey, if that's something you care about, too, then come join us—as a team member *or* a customer." Movement Mortgage is aware that being transparent about their mission and how they use their money helps them attract like-minded people as customers *and* team members.

Leading with mission is less likely to attract a new hire who isn't aligned with organizational goals and focus. Transparency during the hiring and onboarding process helps people learn about what an organization truly values. When candidates know what a company really stands for, they can determine whether it matches their own personal values. Transparency and alignment stem from a clear mission. Getting clarity on mission and what people are working toward is a foundational part of an organization that matters to its people.

Cultural shifts are always dependent on variables specific to each organization. There's no single solution for creating a cultural turnover—no universal application for how to wipe away the obsolete practices lurking in organizations. However, once we start, the more adaptive we become and the less frequently we battle with the adaptability paradox.

The most practical step we can take in supporting ongoing cultural shifts within our organizations is to look for what's obsolete. It's time to come to terms with the fact that ideas about work standardized during the first three industrial revolutions are simply not applicable to modern businesses.

If we look inside our organizations, we start to see what no longer serves us. Many sacred "truths" are obsolete in the New Work Exchange. Like the corset, bell bottoms, and polyester track suits, they've had their time—they pop up on occasion to help us look back *at what was,* but that's not to stop us from running toward what is ahead.

IDENTIFYING THE OBSOLETE

Identifying and changing what's obsolete clears the roadblocks that prevent people and organizations from performing at their best. The easiest way to start identifying what's obsolete in our organizations is to audit ourselves. Start with the following questions:

- Where am I experiencing the most friction in my own work?

- What induced me to roll my eyes the most in the last month?

- Where am I finding the most momentum and fulfillment?

- How easy is it to get things done in our organization?

- What are things I wish we'd start, stop, and continue doing to make us better?

In other words, identifying what's obsolete in our organizations starts with making a wish list of what would make work better *for you*—yes, *you*. That might sound or feel selfish at first, but chances are you'll identify some aspects of daily work that are pain points for everybody.

With that list in hand, we can then start to work through some of the processes and practices in our organizations by asking our team members what they experience. Within our teams, we must ask questions that are embedded in some of the scenarios and anecdotes shared in this chapter:

- Where are decisions being made?

- What rules or policies are title centric or time focused?

- Which of the obsolete practices covered in this chapter sound like our organization?

- What types of people are the most successful in our organization—and how are we defining that success?

- How do we measure and gauge productivity and outcomes?

REFRAMING OUR ORGANIZATIONS

Answering these questions is the best way to identify the pain points caused by the cultural hangovers within our organizations. Creating a new framework starts with asking and answering these questions, listening carefully, and analyzing responses. Readiness to tackle these issues is another by-product of a challenging few years—more people want to resolve these issues than allow them to fester.

We don't need to solve every problem immediately. Over time, we bring new team members into our new work cultures, and those people are good fits for our evolving organizations—but we must remember to support them during our ongoing evolution. Change is hard work, and we're relying on our teams to help us fuel change.

You might ask, "But what if our leadership team doesn't want to hear these things? What if they have no interest in cultural turnover and decentralizing decisions?" Well, *they will likely say that*, so use it as a part of your plan. I always plan ahead when I try to tackle such big issues. In this case, I think a juxtaposition of two company trajectories could be useful. For example: "Did you know Target and Kmart were founded in the exact same year, 1962? We need to be more like Target than Kmart."

It doesn't always feel this way, but all too often *we are* the breakthrough our organizations need! When we spot how our organizations have succumbed to the adaptability paradox, when we become aware of where our policies or cultural approach dictate how we function (or don't function), then we can begin the important work to change it.

> When we become aware of where our policies or cultural approach dictate how we function (or don't function), then we can begin the important work to change it.

People in every role can lead by example by employing these tactics individually, among our teams, and across our organizations. People are more engaged when we leverage our influence to nurture change. No one likes the unknown, and we hate disruption because it causes discomfort. But we can assuage the fear of change by pointing out how other past changes have improved the workplace. Most organizations have had some changes at some point—moving to a new building, upgrading machinery or software, or adding new products and services. When leaders start associating change with *good* outcomes, they are more open to more of them. Sometimes *we* must become change agents.

CHAPTER 4

Putting People First

There's a theme you may have noticed across this book so far: the New Work Exchange is, in almost every way, about people. It's paramount that we work each day with a focus on each other, on people. To build profitable, resilient, innovative organizations, we must nurture the people who bring our businesses alive. So why is it that my chapter about focusing on people is halfway through this book? So glad you asked.

There are reasons change is notoriously difficult. Change isn't linear. In the late 1970s and early 1980s, psychologists James Prochaska, PhD, and Carlo DiClemente, PhD, published research into what became the "transtheoretical model of behavior change," also known as the *stages of change.* The model led to the 1994 book *Changing for Good.* While my summary here is simplified, their theory highlights that change is hard *because* there are stages of change. By failing to understand or recognize the stages, we lose momentum forward.

Their model includes six stages of change: precontemplation, contemplation, preparation, action, maintenance, and relapse. Between stages of change, there's also a potential to relapse and rely on old behaviors—that adaptability paradox is a powerful force! However, we can also learn from relapses, and the learning process fuels an *upward spiral* to the next level of change.

Exactly as it sounds, in the precontemplation phase, people aren't ready to even think about change. In the contemplation phase, we're aware of problems, but we're *just thinking* about change. Then we get ready for change in the preparation stage. Only after we've moved through these three stages do we *act* to modify or adapt behaviors.

You may be thinking this model is about personal behavior, not organizations or businesses, so what does it have to do with the New Work Exchange? *People are at the core of our organizations.* If personal, behavioral change occurs in stages, and our organizations operate because of people, then why would we think change within our organizations would happen any differently? The New Work Exchange will only occur through stages of change—and each of us has a mission to do our part to speed this along.

Furthermore, if we want our organizations to change and adapt, then wouldn't we need to equip people to grow and change? To thrive organizationally, we need our people to thrive. For organizations to pivot into this new era of work, we need people and organizations to align more closely. Another word for alignment is *change.* Our organizations need to change—we need to align with what people have been asking for so they can engage at work. We need more people to accept and embrace this new era of work, *and* we need to work together to fully enable the New Work Exchange. That's layers of change, and at the heart of it all are people.

Up to this point, I've shared how work got to this point in time. In doing so, we've been thinking about change and getting ready for change. We've been, in many ways, identifying our roadblocks by asking, "What's standing in our way?" The recurring theme has been the need to recognize people and their value as more important than standardization of practice or managerial style. In many ways, *we've* been standing in our own way, perhaps stunted by the comfort of a well-organized policy manual that spells out what's important.

We're standing on the edge of something new and different, and with that comes new options and new possibilities. If we're ever going to push for change in our organizations, now is the time to do so! We must commit to actively changing how we approach the people at the core of our organizations. Simply *saying* people come first hasn't resulted in transformation. It's time to *put people first* to create the changes we need within our organizations. In this chapter, we'll explore ways of doing just that.

> Simply saying people come first hasn't resulted in transformation. It's time to put people first to create the changes we need within our organizations.

It's important to realize there are times—no matter how much experience we have—when we benefit from embracing a learner's mindset. We don't know everything. To evolve, we must learn new things. On the journey of the New Work Exchange, I remind myself to be a constant learner. That's doubly true regarding people. It's possible to learn from everyone. When we enable people to drive decision-making within our organizations, it becomes crucial to adopt active listening, broader awareness, and learning skills. Regardless of title, tenure, or role, a curious mindset helps us engage with the world and team members.

As we embark on creating lasting change in our organizations, let's start with an important question: At work, do you see colleagues and employees, *or* do you see *people*?

REFLECTING: NEW TEAMS AND ORGANIZATIONS

Joining a new organization is always exciting, but you never really know what you're going to get until you get started. I once accepted a new position and looked forward to participating in what was supposed to be a highly energized and focused team. In my first few weeks, I saw something different. The team was deeply divided on what was best for the organization. To make matters worse, there were two unwritten rules affecting everyone: conflicts were to be avoided, and we had to "fake it till we make it."

An unintended outcome of not having a healthy level of conflict was that too many aspects of the business could easily be hidden, which meant they weren't dealt with promptly. Ignoring pain points had become a coping mechanism with each meeting, report, and conversation, so many people were completely unaware of the peril facing the organization. What seemed to matter most was that we "looked the part."

At my first executive leadership team meeting, I came with my business face on, wanting nothing more than to be a bridge to take the team from its existing state to a new and improved one. I was ready to be a change agent and focus on business problems. Instead, I entered a conference room and found people chatting about their personal lives.

My increasing anxiety about the organization's lack of apparent desire to confront its issues pushed me over the edge. As our executive team discussed the banana bread they were passing around the table, I suddenly blurted out, "Someone tell me about this organization's culture!"

Heads went down; forced smiles were frozen on faces. An awkward silence overcame the room, and no one said a word. The rest of the meeting went from bad to worse. After the meeting, I asked one of my colleagues to stop by my office so I could get feedback about the meeting. That is, I was ready to have a meeting after the meeting.

Expecting to talk about the disastrous meeting and the state of the business, their first comment took me by complete surprise:

"You haven't even asked me about my cats," they said.

"Your cats?" I asked. As I posed my question, my face contorted itself into what felt like a mask with the same fake, awkward smile I'd seen on people's faces during the meeting. My discomfort was surely visible.

My colleague pointed out that the briefing I'd received about the executive team included a mention of their cats who were like their children. And since I'd joined the company, I'd not asked about their cats.

Should I have asked about the cats? Yes, I should have. But I didn't realize this until well after the fact.

Believe me, I get how easy it is to roll our eyes at examples like this. But I'd asked about culture in frustration when there were signs of the organization's culture all around me, including the banana bread. Having gone into the meeting with my own agenda, I'd bristled against what my colleagues were focused on. At the time, the organization focused heavily on the personal aspects of work—I'd had my game face on to focus on business. It was the first of many lessons I needed to learn on the art and science of aligning people and organizations in meaningful ways.

Andy Warhol once said, "Being good in business is the most fascinating kind of art. Making money is art and working is art and good business is the best art."[22] Good business is helping an organization achieve its potential. To do that, people within organizations must achieve their potential. Work is part science, part art. Soon after my failed meeting, I realized my approach had been wrong for the transformation underway at the organization. I'd been too focused on the science of business—and not enough on the art of people. The gift I learned was that people and business aren't at odds—rather, they are a balancing act required for success.

Extremes of any kind in business are usually a trap, whether that's time and focus we give to the business or the people in our business. Balance is what we're striving toward.

The dynamic between people and business isn't a problem to solve. Rather, it's a state of evolution that we must continually nurture and manage. Why? Both are always changing and adapting to the world around them. By incorporating human beings into our organizations instead of focusing on employees, we're more attuned to the changes taking place at every level of work. It also creates trust, which leads to more transparency in what's working and not working for people—and that's always great for business and people.

LEADING *WITH* PEOPLE

As we've talked about, we're experiencing the Fourth Industrial Revolution. Let's think of it as Work 4.0. Establishing new ways of working, adapting expectations, and setting new underlying themes are all paramount to our success in Work 4.0. For a moment, let's go back to Thomas's classic book *Intrinsic Motivation at Work*. In the book, he outlines that as work evolved, "We began 'enriching' workers' jobs in the 1970s. Then we 'empowered' workers in the 1980s and 1990s. And now that the work is more demanding and there is looser supervision, we need to make sure that workers are psychologically 'engaged' in performing that work." [23]

For the past two decades, organizations have talked a lot about employee engagement, which is at the heart of Thomas's book. Understanding people's motivations establishes engagement—right? After more than twenty years, we're still *talking* about engagement but seem to have made little progress in *engaging* our employees. According to Gallup's *State of the Global Workplace: 2022 Report*, "Global employee vital signs—*engagement* and well-being—remain stable but not great." An indicator of underwhelming vitals is that only 21 percent of employees across the globe are engaged at work.[24] We started focusing on engagement years ago, so why are we still struggling to crack the code on it?

Perhaps we skipped something vital: to motivate people at work, you have to start by focusing on *people*. The full person comes to work, not just the *worker*. Research from McKinsey highlights what they describe as "the need for a genuine, personalized, and multidimensional employee experience." They indicate that to "create the human-centered experience people are craving," it's vital to recognize that employee engagement is primarily driven by nonfinancial recognition. Their top recommendation for human-centered experience is, well, to put people first.

Personalizing relationships and avoiding a transactional approach as part of work is what people need, want, and are asking for, even though many common and current tactics are actually, "transactional, commonplace, and impersonal."[25] There's a time and a place for a transactional job. When it comes to our careers and work that we care about—and will be psychologically engaged with—it's fundamental that our relationship with our employer be more than transactional. Alignment between person and organization requires we move beyond the transaction with the *worker*.

Tacking on to concepts so adroitly articulated by Thomas two decades ago, the evolution of work has catapulted organizations through eras and trends at work. After focusing on *enriching* and *empowering*, we pivoted to *engaging*. We've struggled to engage at work because we've avoided embracing *people* and are overdue in embracing the changes in front of us. Postpandemic, it's not enough to *engage workers*. It's time to build relationships, personalize experiences, and *lead with people*.

CREATING PEOPLE EXPERIENCES

We can *create* Work 4.0 rather than just *react* to it—adapting how we define the when, why, how, and where of work. At the center of that is—and should be—the daily experience people have at work.

> We can keep managing projects, timelines, and processes, but let's make the shift to leading with people.

Contemplate the employee experience at your organization, then think about *your* experience at work. How do you impact people's work experiences through actions, policies, workstyles, and habits? What's required for your business to become people centric? We can keep managing projects, timelines, and processes, but let's make the shift to leading with people.

Unlike any other resource, people are inspired to do great work, both for individual achievement and the collective good. We experience; we don't just produce. People are a *human resource*, which is why organizations evolved to have a department known as human resources (HR). People within organizations carry and produce a unique form of value known as human capital—the value an individual's or group's skills, knowledge, and experience bring to an organization.

For a thoughtfully designed human experience within an organization—one that is personalized, targeted, strategic, and engaging—we must create intentional human capital management strategies. Our strategies must underscore how we find, hire, support, and retain people. Understanding and designing for human capital effectiveness is a *must have* for positive, tailored experiences in the New Work Exchange.

This requires seeing each person at work as an individual who can elevate the human capital value within an organization. For emphasis, a person's value isn't the work *produced for* a company. Creating an ideal experience for people at work requires understanding that people will always have human needs that are more important than their roles as employees. The goal isn't to force a choice between a person's needs and their work but to facilitate both.

When we have empathy for an individual's life situation, we tend to help them as a person. That empathy shouldn't be turned off when we come to work. It becomes everyone's responsibility to accept that exceptions aren't the exception, and that's a foundational element of business. As Anne M. Mulcahy, the former CEO of Xerox, expressed: "Employees who believe that management is concerned about them as a whole person—not just an employee—are more productive, more satisfied, more fulfilled. Satisfied employees mean satisfied customers, which leads to profitability."[26]

It's imperative that we have highly diverse, people-centric rewards programs that help people live the life they want. Now when I say rewards, I'm not speaking in general terms—instead, I'm calling on a particular form of the term regularly used by human resources, compensation, and benefits practitioners. Without going too far down a specific professional track, understanding what WorldatWork refers to as Total Rewards™ helps build meaningful experiences *for people* at work.

At WorldatWork, we're committed to Total Rewards—also just referred to as rewards—because they recognize how a personalized approach to supporting people is a differentiator at work. A strategic program for rewards leads to people who are more productive, inspired, and committed at work, which results in expanded capabilities and improved overall performance. I'm going to take that a step further, though. Total Rewards are a defining and critical element in *making work better*. A well-designed program offers an array of rewards for different purposes, leveraged in the right way to appeal to a variety of human needs.

UNDERSTANDING REWARDS

The New Work Exchange requires a fair, comprehensive, thoughtful, people-centric, and responsive strategy for Total Rewards. Work isn't *just* about monetary compensation. Total Rewards is a practice for rewarding, compensating, focusing, and enabling people to function and thrive, *even when* exceptions happen in life. To this end, a thoughtful rewards strategy underscores that an organization recognizes people's value.

> A thoughtful rewards strategy underscores that an organization recognizes people's value.

Rewards require that we consider, strategize, and deliver on people's needs, which makes them an active practice within an organization as opposed to a static offering. Strong rewards strategies reflect the changing priorities of people within an organization, which facilitates overall business impact and better outcomes. Seen in this way, Total Rewards are a way to effectively lead and align people and organizations. Rewards are a contemporary language for people experiences and business performance.

At WorldatWork, we have entire courses that instruct on the nuances and specifics of rewards, so I'm not going to get academic here. We believe there are elements of rewards people need at work *and* to improve work. Once we recognize people at the center of work, it's paramount to start building work experiences for people. What's offered as part of a rewards program conveys an organization's culture, style, priorities, and overall alignment. In many ways, rewards are the ultimate opportunity to signal an organization's culture—existing or emerging—to prospective and existing team members.

The elements of Total Rewards include compensation, benefits, well-being, development, and recognition. However, as anyone who works knows, there are a lot of influencers that shape these elements as well. How we balance the art and science of rewards should reflect our people. Building positive work experiences means tailoring our approach to these elements, which you'll see reflected in the specific steps suggested below. Rather than focusing on the explicit list of rewards elements, I've sought to bring their meaning and impact to life. As we consider the following tips, it's critical to remember that we can't reward people if we are focused on "workers" instead of *people*.

VISUALIZING THE IDEAL EMPLOYEE EXPERIENCE

That's right—time to get out the vision board. It's not enough to just encourage employees to bring their full selves to work every day and engage in collaboration. Good culture and experience don't come from chance—they don't just *happen* but rather are deliberately made. Visualize what an ideal employee experience would look like at your organization. Design it. Put it in place.

The ideal employee experience is a mission we can work toward. We all contribute to employee experience. And guess what? An organization's approach to Total Rewards must *fit into, help shape, and round out overall employee experience.*

> **An organization's approach to Total Rewards must fit into, help shape, and round out overall employee experience.**

Regardless of our roles in the workplace, we all interact with colleagues. What do you want your interactions to be like? If you have a team, what do you want the people you lead to experience at work as a direct result of your efforts? If you are part of a human resources, compensation, or benefits team, what's your organization's strategy for elevating the employee experience?

Jot down some ideas based on your visualizations, and then start testing them with different people to see how it goes. That's right—we're allowed to experiment before we make sweeping changes!

Experiment with flipping the norms on traditional methods of decision-making, protocol, or processes. Develop new programs. Rethink your programs for compensation, benefits, and well-being. Get to the root of equity, belonging, diversity, and inclusion within your company by establishing committees and sponsoring a consultant to help with an organizational DEI audit. Suggest a formal pay equity assessment.

In all cases, document the changes and results. How are your engagement rates—did they change? Did work get done faster or slower? Was friction reduced? What was the impact on emotional well-being and confidence across the team? Have customer satisfaction numbers changed?

Workplaces can and should be a place of learning, but that's only possible if we constantly try new things and adapt old ones. It'd be great if this all was super easy and led to organizations having big "kumbaya" moments. What it generally leads to are moments of breakthrough that build on each other until there is a palpable difference in people's daily experiences.

Here are a few critical ways to shape employee experience.

INTEGRATE LIFE INTENTIONALLY

When Indra Nooyi became CEO at Pepsi, her approach to life outside the company influenced her organization's culture. "At the end of the day, don't forget you're a person," she said, "don't forget you're a mother, don't forget you're a wife, don't forget you're a daughter."[27]

By emphasizing that she was a person first, she opened the door for other employees to integrate their personal lives more intentionally into their work. Nooyi's approach was relatively unheard of for CEOs, especially in the world of Fortune 500s. By bringing her full self and true priorities along to work with her in such a public way, she made it OK for others at Pepsi to do the same. A new standard was set.

We should all follow suit. It changes an organization's fabric, making work and workplaces inherently more *human*. We can't build rewards for people unless we're integrating life into our organizations.

ONBOARD DELIBERATELY

Intentionally design recruiting and onboarding processes. Often these processes get adapted as different people work on them—too often at the last minute—and over time that results in discombobulation.

Hiring processes should be transparent, organized, easy, fast, impactful, and inclusive. Most hiring and onboarding processes lack a focused strategic goal. This is a missed opportunity. Carefully write an employee value statement that outlines the organization's desired employee experience. Onboarding should prepare a new person for what they need to know as they contemplate joining a team.

> **The key outcome of a successful onboarding program is that you facilitate the process of a new hire going from an outsider to an insider.**

Also, be fully transparent during orientation programs to reinforce that people are at the center of your business. Onboarding is a perfect time to outline stakeholders and the larger ecosystem that works together to drive results. The key outcome of a successful onboarding program is that you facilitate the process of a new hire going from an outsider to an insider because that is where they'll ultimately do their best work.

Use these processes to truly engage the people going through them, including seeking feedback on products, processes, or even the company brand. In other words, stop hiring people and *telling* them what to do. Instead, hire them, and have them provide feedback on things they've observed, seen, and experienced. New hires can provide perspective that only a fresh set of eyes can see.

Whenever we have a new hire on board, I set up time to meet with that person within their first few weeks on the team, and these conversations have been some of the most productive I've had as a CEO. I try to make sure our chat isn't too early in a person's tenure but when they've had a chance to start seeing patterns in their experiences and are primed to provide feedback. These chats are also a critical first step toward helping people belong and setting the expectation their involvement is truly valued and rewarded.

REINFORCE ACTIVELY

Make sure people are fully trained on and excited about the desired employee experience so everyone partakes in it and fulfills its design. Managers must figure out ways to bring a vision to life, even during inconvenient times. It's not enough to have a vision for employee experience.

If organizations promise missions, experiences, or sets of values but don't fulfill them, people will figure out the contradictions quickly. It's both costly and aggravating for new hires when they're told an organization is flexible, but their manager scolds them for using that flexibility.

DESIGN FOR IMPACT

Be as specific as you can about where a person can likely make their biggest impact within an organization, including the good they may do in their role. Every new hire can be given multiple ways to have early wins, which helps both their onboarding and their confidence.

Set people up for success from the moment they join your organization. People like to work with organizations that win, so don't be shy about sharing your success, especially if you've been able to create good in the world while also hitting your consecutive quarterly goals.

BECOME A STUDENT OF HUMAN BEHAVIOR

People are daunting. We can be reactionary and emotional, and we are always learning. But in some ways, we can also be reluctant to learn, which makes leading people and fostering positive outcomes challenging. Behavior that's happened at work literally feeds talk-show hosts and comedians, who poke fun at outrageous bosses or other things that fit under the category "You would not believe what happened at work today."

These examples are anecdotal but relevant. There was the telecom executive team that released a company-wide memo indicating internal communication was a problem but that "the company would not be discussing it." Another manager asked an employee for a report on a project they were leading—when the employee asked if they could submit it first thing the next morning, the manager quipped back, "If I wanted it tomorrow, I'd have asked you tomorrow." My personal favorite was when a C-suite leader asked that email stop being used to pass on information or data since it was restricted to "company business."

Most of the time, scenarios like this happen at work because individuals or groups of people are trying to avoid getting too close to human behavior. In an attempt at sidestepping the very elements that make us human—particularly emotions—it's common to try to avoid *people*. At such moments, we overfocus on the organization, hierarchy, and process. But those are the very moments that help us become students of human behavior, which improves culture at work as well as our ability to lead teams.

Sometimes we complicate this thing called human behavior, so let's look at a few things we *know* about people. Regardless of where you live or what you do, people are social beings. As a fundamental aspect of being human, we need to *belong*.

How does your organization foster belonging? How do *you*? Much of this book is about helping people be themselves and feel like they belong where they work. This could be taking steps to open communication, being more transparent, starting employee interest groups, increasing transparency, and empowering people to do what they were hired to do and then some.

We do our best when we are a part of a community, which is being a part of something bigger than our individual selves. Organizations are strong centers for creating communities united in a vision and outlook. Phrases like "It's business, not personal" have overstayed their welcome. Too often, we rely on tropes such as these when we need to do hard things that involve people. Business *is* personal—work *is* personal. That's precisely why we must reset *how* we work and reward people.

Business is personal—work is personal. That's precisely why we must reset how we work and reward people.

For a strong, healthy sense of self, people need to feel they're supported, can speak their minds, and are heard. Agency within organizations fuels a sense of empowerment and strength—for individuals and teams. Part of leading is making sure people feel a sense of maximum belonging. People are reluctant, if not resistant, to do their best work if they aren't supported as people. When people are treated like *employees* who are replaceable and just provide a function, it influences and guides their behavior at work. No matter what an organization does or produces, people are the central figures in that business.

People don't just bring their bodies to work—they bring their minds, ideas, and behaviors. That means all these aspects that come to work with a person are a *part of work*. Everyone is slightly different— we all have our own quirks, which also come to work. By focusing on a person's higher-level traits, we find ways to engage and understand each other, which facilitates becoming a student of common behaviors and communication styles.

There are a variety of ways we can create more formal profiles for ourselves and our teams to better bridge how we work together. Self-assessments such as the DiSC, Meyers-Briggs, or the Enneagram personality tests are all options I've seen teams make good use of—it doesn't matter what test is used as long as it provides insight into engaging with various personalities and behaviors while leaving room for flexibility on the individual level.

Understanding behavior requires us to recognize that there are five generations in the workforce today: traditionalists, boomers, Generation X, millennials, and Generation Z. The way these groups approach work is different—not to mention that the ways they employ and are comfortable with technology span from "digital nomads" to "digital no-thanks."

The more we can understand and witness what makes us different, the more we can find our commonalities. However, this requires us to put in the work to understand the people with whom we work. This may seem overwhelming at first, but it'll save time and energy in the longer term when insights can be used to enhance productivity or engagement.

DEVELOPING FLEXIBILITY

Despite what we've been taught, work doesn't have to be monotonous. In the era of Work 4.0 and the New Work Exchange, we must ask ourselves if we value people's time in the way *they* value it. In the Old Work Exchange, the company set the value of time. We have an opportunity to value time based on what people value, which requires our flexibility.

This requires a shift away from absolutist, right-or-wrong, black-or-white, yes-or-no thinking and toward a continuum that reflects people's changing needs. Something like getting to work late *could* be wrong, especially if a manufacturing line is held up. However, unless a job explicitly hinges on shift work, is it possible to focus on the impact to the team and customer? Such an approach removes the right-or-wrong element of the behavior and elevates a coachable moment, so it's likely to get more traction.

> **Focus on ways to relieve the pressure of work—which often amounts to scheduling—and replace it with new options for getting work done.**

Flexibility creates trust. When we stop trying to control the way work gets done, people have an increased amount of agency with their work. Focus on ways to relieve the pressure of work—which often amounts to scheduling—and replace it with new options for getting work done.

There are many creative ways to build flexibility into teams and organizations. Many of them relate back to rewards programs. For example, Netflix doesn't track their employees' hours or their PTO—they work when they want, and the company only measures their output. Netflix calls this their "No Vacation Policy." This includes giving people unlimited parental leave since some families need more time to adjust to a new child than others. Consider the family with a newborn in neonatal intensive care. It's unlikely a traditional parental leave would cover situations that lead to long hospitalizations—and it's even more unlikely people would be productive if they were forced to return to work while they are stressed out about their child's well-being.

Now, I know what you're thinking: "Scott, we're not a huge company like Netflix." But Netflix has had this policy since there were fewer than one hundred people on the team.[28] Through WorldatWork's research on Total Rewards practices, we've seen a growing percentage of organizations—from 8 percent in 2016 to 17 percent in 2021—offering unlimited PTO, which shows the trend is catching on and making an impact.[29]

Not ready for unlimited PTO? Fine. What about offering paid sabbaticals to help your team members avoid burnout? According to a recent WorldatWork article on *Workspan Daily*, it's an approach that Salesloft, Intel, Adobe, and McDonald's have implemented.[30]

There are also plenty of other ways to be flexible: dress code, work schedule, pay dates, work location, and work types. Unilever's U-Work program gives contract employees the freedom and flexibility of gig work but also covers them with job security and benefits.[31]

Think about it: How could flexibility benefit *your company?* How could flexibility benefit *you* at work?

ENCOURAGE STEWARDSHIP

Organizations should be full of stewards. Too many opportunities are missed when people are told—or tell each other—to "stay in their lane." Whether you've caught yourself saying it, heard colleagues saying it, or realized your organization's onboarding and training encourages people to remain focused on the roles for which they were hired, it's time to influence change.

We rarely contribute ideas that drive innovation or improve a project if we all have blinders on. Focus is important, and we all need rules of engagement, but we also need *collaboration*. Encourage hidden potential, tap it, and help people grow projects and businesses. This also means people are challenged to step outside their comfort zones to find new ways they can contribute as stakeholders, which we'll discuss more in the next chapter.

One of my favorite tactics for this is encouraging people to find "jobbies." When people get to combine things they love—a hobby—with something they can get paid or rewarded for—a job—then it's a nice hybrid opportunity. For most people, it's a sweet spot that emphasizes their value, leverages their skills, and integrates them as stakeholders. This approach is a defining element of great places to work.

Jobbies not only make people feel important, but they also check off multiple boxes in the New Work Exchange. Engagement increases when we allow people to be their full selves, contribute talents that benefit the whole organization, and sharpen a skill for which they are paid. From my experience, everyone does better when they find a jobbie that works for them and a company.

BUILDING RECOGNITION AND APPRECIATION

One of the reasons I love Total Rewards is that they help people and organizations unlock their work potential and achieve fulfilling lives. Think about it—every major life event people have can be supported and facilitated by a Total Rewards program: Benefits that enable managing the cost of having a child, paid time off to celebrate an anniversary, a bonus that helps with the purchase of a new home, the

401(k) that secures a great retirement, the recognition that makes a person feel confident.

How do you strategically celebrate a milestone or achievement in a worker's personal life? The Old Work Exchange honored tenure above everything else, so many workplaces only celebrate milestone anniversaries for how long a person has worked for a company. If coworkers have bandwidth for it, we might celebrate birthdays, but that's challenging with more people working remotely. Whatever we choose, it should scream, "We value you!"

When we start understanding that the whole person comes to work, we can recognize and appreciate people differently. What might matter to people? People care about the black belt in karate they've been working toward for years. Or how about when their child graduates as the class valedictorian? What if someone finally earns a degree that took years of night classes or they publish a book? Someone in your organization has probably won a local award for their volunteering efforts or placed first in their community's local casserole competition.

In the pursuit of work-life harmony and greater integration of the full self at work, it's important to find what makes your people "shine" and then find ways to bring that shine into our organizations. And yes, people love their cats, and when you can, it's great to ask about them.

Again, I know this sounds like a lot of work. However, good dialogue in our organizations increases the likelihood that we'll learn about these important moments in people's lives, be able to recognize them, and go on to appreciate them. Don't be like the company I mentioned earlier with the mandatory Employee Appreciation Day that employees had to pay to attend.

Also, we can do better than the way a fast-food company celebrated a team member who had never missed a day of work in his twenty-seven years of work. For all that time and dedication, management gave him a bag with a movie ticket, coffee cup, and candy. The uninspiring moment was captured on video and went viral on social media. Why? For most, it was an example of how organizations miss opportunities to recognize and reward people thoughtfully. It was a real "Guess what happened at work today?" moment.

In fact, the "recognition" left so many people shaking their heads that a GoFundMe page was set up for the team member. The hope was to raise $200 for his years of service. Instead, the effort raised almost $300,000. When the employee asked what he'd do with the money, he said he'd visit his grandkids and maybe set up a college fund, but otherwise, "I'm just working."[32] Whatever route you take, be authentic, and find the time to make the moment matter to your people, and then do all you can to elevate it.

CULTIVATING GROWTH

Providing growth opportunities is an essential way to invest and reinvest in our team members. People have an innate need to learn, adapt, and grow. A lack of growth opportunities regularly registers as one of the top reasons workers leave organizations. People development is a part of *everyone's job*, not just HR's. Having people complete the annual mandatory safety training or sexual harassment seminar isn't the same as providing ongoing growth. Part of the reason people are "quietly quitting" is that they are bored with their roles and are using the time to invest in themselves.

Cultivating growth opportunities starts when we hire. A job description may be the initial attractor and an indication of what the person will focus on for a limited time. But the speed of business and human development means that job descriptions may be relevant only for a short time. The knowledge, skills, and abilities—for today's job and the future—should be included in hiring profiles within organizations. Employers need to encourage people to apply to roles, even when they don't believe they are a one-to-one match for the specified job requirements. People should grow into roles, *and organizations should encourage that growth routinely.*

Contemporary practices can borrow something from the past to help us: apprenticeships. Historically, such programs have been incredibly important for teaching new skills and trades. In the United States, the National Apprenticeship Act was signed into law in 1937, outlining regulations and safety protocols.[33] However, you can borrow the concept of teaching by using mentoring, job-share, or even job-shadowing programs that transfer skills and insights to others. The only feasible way we can grow skills at the pace demanded by this accelerated world is to find ways to train on the job and in every workplace.

Spend time assessing how we can invest in people *inside* our organizations. Expose people to opportunities in organizations by creating growth tracks and programs, including learning opportunities like webinars or conferences. Allow individuals to shadow people or teams, including leaders. This kind of future-oriented cross-training not only upskills people but also upskills a company.

Then look for ways to foster growth outside the organization. This could include volunteer opportunities for team building or even lending out executives to local nonprofits for small projects or consultations. Hire retired people as interns and teach them new skills or build returnship programs in which people with decades of experience mentor emerging talent.

Growth in human capital is the key to driving financial growth. Too often, when organizations discuss growth, we're focused on financial capital. Given the intense speed of business, many organizations would benefit from acting more like start-ups. With the hurdles we all face, we'd also benefit from acting like educational training organizations that constantly update their most critical resource—people.

PRIORITIZING WELL-BEING

We have an opportunity to shift away from traditional approaches to offering medical, dental, and vision benefits to a more well-rounded approach. Well-being programs consider the well-rounded needs of individuals and families. Aristotle referred to well-being (*eudaimonia*) as the state of humans flourishing and living well.[34] In contemporary settings, we define well-being as the state in which people are happy, healthy, and prosperous.

Well-being benefits range from mental-health support, diversity and inclusion programs, telemedicine, physical health, nutrition programs, vaccinations, nap rooms, or any program that supports the whole person who works. One of the most impactful ways a company can go beyond commercialized well-being programs is to create a more diverse and inclusive work environment. People need space for the social issues they care about.

Some organizations offer courses on being creative, having conversations with teenagers, eating well, and even investment essentials. The important part is to look at the wider team to determine a responsive, personalized approach to what people within our organizations need and want—this step is critical in creating alignment with people.

At WorldatWork, we see companies looking to positively impact the biggest stressors people experience—generally finances, parenting, relationships—by providing resources designed to support people. Some organizations provide this through courses and workshops; others use Employee Assistance Programs (EAPs), or supplementary benefits packages that provide online therapy. Other organizations create diversity initiatives, such as Employee Resource Groups (ERGs), in which they can connect with others from similar backgrounds. Another popular option for organizations not ready for unlimited PTO is the PTO bank, to which employees can donate unused time off for other team members to use.[35] But the most effective organization makes space for these life challenges in the work experience itself.

Well-being comes in many shapes and sizes. Biopharmaceutical company AbbVie decided to train all their managers to recognize unconscious bias against women. The goal was to prevent bias from happening in the first place. Not only does this create a more equitable workplace and improve personal well-being, but it also improves the company's well-being.

ESTABLISHING EQUITY

Recently, a senior travel reporter from The Points Guy resigned and posted her salary online. Her message to anyone hired was to demand no less than $115,000, a signing bonus, and—if they were asked to move—a relocation package. She revealed that she had been making $107,000, and after learning what some of her colleagues were making, she found her salary unfair.[36]

In other words, when companies don't volunteer transparency, employees will do it for them. These steps facilitate stakeholder-ship and equity for those who replace them. There's nothing wrong with being fully transparent about pay ranges and salaries—and it's perfectly legal for current and past employees to discuss their salaries if they choose. Organizations must accept that it will become increasingly normalized for people to have these discussions. If organizations aren't paying equitably or fairly, they'll be publicly called out for it. And when that happens, it's a risk the organization took by design. If that's not a risk you're willing to take—and I recommend it shouldn't be—then our only recourse is to be proactive, fair, and transparent with how we design and deliver compensation programs.

We've got significant problems to confront when people feel they need to leave an organization—and publicly reveal information about the experience of working there—to attempt to influence equity and transparency in their wake. It's time to move beyond the optics to make the changes we are espousing.

The pressure to focus on and deliver equitable workplaces hasn't abated since the pandemic—it's increased, which will only continue due to a confluence of factors. So it's important for organizations to have compensation philosophies and practices ensuring that people are paid fairly for the work they do. To deliver on equitable pay, we must look beyond pay exclusively.

In Syndio's *2023 Workplace Equity Trends Report*, the company clarifies that *workplace equity* is more than just *pay equity*. The report outlines how equity must be embedded in all aspects of the employment journey—information and analysis empower a comprehensive approach to equity practices that fuels alignment between a company and its people.

In the report, they identified several aspects of workplace equity that are crucial to analyze: workforce composition, diversity benchmarking, recruitment, performance, promotions and movement, engagement, attrition, *and* pay equity. A key takeaway of their report is that it's no longer enough to conduct a once-a-year equity "audit."

Instead, organizations require a comprehensive strategy that supports a practice of ongoing analysis to ensure workplace equity is embedded as part of how the company operates. "The root causes of inequity don't hit the pause button after closing out an annual pay equity analysis. That's why one of the most fundamental shifts that Syndio is seeing is a move to more frequent pay equity analyses …

By shifting from a reactive, point-in-time correction [audit] to an ongoing, proactive adjustment process, organizations can more easily stay on top of the state of equity in their company."[37]

There's a lot of discussion about whether to publish job postings with salaries or disclose what people earn within an organization. Some states have legislated that job posts must show a salary range. The goals with these shifts are trust, fairness, transparency, and equitable practices within organizations. If we don't, people will publicly reveal how our vision, mission, and goal statements are just that—statements without substance.

DELIVERING SUBSTANCE

Look up from the book or device on which you are reading, and peer into the future. Start to visualize what work could look and feel like. What's your ideal state of work? How can you use your skills to influence and create that state? Be bold with your vision. How impactful could a few of these changes be for you, your teams, colleagues, and even your organization? Always remember that work and life aren't at odds—they're intertwined, and there's no way to separate them.

In the New Work Exchange, we have a challenge in front of us: determining what we *truly do value most* and then following through with the change required to reinforce what we most value. That requires us to do more than just *say* we value people but *demonstrate* the ways in which we value people.

Whatever your role—you may be a team leader, manager, executive leader, human resources professional, or an individual contributor—you have an opportunity in your slice of the workplace to make the experience more human and more valuable to the people with whom you interact. Whether those interactions are in person or on a screen from a thousand miles away, how we approach each other matters. How we demonstrate value to each other matters.

When people provide their time and expertise, they should earn respect, inclusion, and a paved career path. Supporting people should include cool perks, well-being, development, and growth. We all impact one another, so why not maximize that impact?

The experiences people have at work must be suggested, designed, and implemented. Experiences only happen when we see an opportunity, are ready for change, and *make the change.* If it's not in your role to design or influence compensation programs, it may be in your sphere of influence to recognize or informally nominate a colleague for a reward after you've seen them go above and beyond.

Perhaps you want to suggest or be involved in an Employee Resource Group (ERG) which would impact your organizational culture. If you are an HR, compensation, or benefits specialist, you could suggest that your organization assess its approach to Total Rewards. Or you may be the leader in an organization who wants to take a position on pay transparency. Whatever the case may be, we all contribute to the New Work Exchange.

By recognizing human capital as our greatest and most important resource, we can act on the opportunity to make work better. Influencing, impacting, and designing ways to support and reward people at work are tremendous opportunities. When we all embrace how we contribute to change, we become part of a great legacy that ultimately makes the world a better place to work.

CHAPTER 5

Fostering Stakeholders

When people are engaged, inspired, committed, and productive at work, they tend to feel included and valued. There's an understanding that they matter and their work matters, and their work influences outcomes.

Recently, during an interview with a candidate that was going swimmingly well—there was obvious alignment on both sides, organizational and individual—I metaphorically handed the keys over to the candidate to drive the conversation once all my questions were answered. It's important to have people interview organizations as much as we're interviewing them. Hiring is a *two-way* conversation.

After the candidate asked her questions, I asked if there was anything I could clarify or explain. The reply was interesting. "I'm all in!" she said.

I felt as though I understood the candidate's meaning, but I also wanted to make sure I wasn't incorrectly reading enthusiasm, so I decided to ask for clarity. She replied, "I mean I'm all in. I buy in. I'm committed. From all my research and all my interviews, it's clear there's something special here, and I want to be a part of it. I can grow here. I can influence things here."

This candidate epitomized a stakeholder mindset. She wanted to join a team that valued her *and her desire* to be more than a worker. She wanted to be—and be recognized as—a stakeholder in any organization she joined. Not only were her skills a great fit for the role we had, but her approach to work also aligned with ours.

The New Work Exchange requires businesses to become more people centric. Everything within organizations, including results and outcomes, is elevated when we see our team members as people and then understand their roles as our most important stakeholders. Across this chapter, we'll look at what that means and why it's so important.

REFLECTING: GOOD SIGNALS AND PRACTICES

When I give speeches, people often come up to me after to share stories about their workplaces. One such time, I was speaking at an event hosted by an organization that had made it onto the list of the best workplaces in the United States. Events like this often attract attendees who want to learn what it takes to be part of or lead a *great workplace.*

During the reception following my speech, a gentleman approached me and shared some stories about his CEO, which I admit were some of the absolute worst I'd ever heard. He shared example after example of exactly what you'd *never* want any CEO to do, including things like making employees declare during all-staff meetings if they were "happy and on the bus" (or not) and publicly declaring PTO as "working from a nicer place."

After several minutes detailing examples of this CEO's behavior, the gentleman asked me if I thought there was hope for him at the organization. That's a big question to place in the hands of a stranger, and despite my sincere desire to help him be an agent of change in his workplace, my instincts kicked in, and I said, "If what you have told me is accurate, I'd run fast and never look back."

Then we shook hands and wished each other well.

A year later, I was recruited and joined a new company. During the interview process, the CEO described the company's "very unique culture." He reinforced how people were at the center of the business, which had an impact on nearly every aspect of their rapidly growing and global organization.

I was extremely excited. Had I found a place that treated employees like people and engaged them as true stakeholders?

Well, the short answer is no.

The CEO who interviewed me wasn't the CEO who came into work during my first week on the job. Yes, it was the same *person*, but he didn't have the same *personality*. Initially, I chalked it up to communication differences—nothing I couldn't adapt to. "Maybe the terms I'm using don't have the same meaning here or with this CEO," I thought.

But nope, that wasn't the case. Remember the gentleman who approached me after my speech? The one with all the scary stories about the CEO? In what may be the most ironic twist of my professional career, I ended up joining *that* exact organization. You know, the organization I suggested he should leave, run from fast, and never look back. Yeah, that one. Without realizing it, I joined *that* company and reported to *that* CEO.

The good news is I'd given the gentleman the absolute right advice. I'd never have pieced the stories together had I not bumped into him at another conference. After he'd heard where I was working, he approached me to ask if I remembered him speaking to me about his CEO. I did remember the conversation, and after experiencing it for myself, I totally got what he'd encountered.

My takeaway from the company: "Very unique culture" doesn't necessarily mean "good" culture. "Unique" can signal a lot. In hindsight, it was code for all the ways the CEO *didn't* want the organization to improve, modernize, or put people first—and the ways people *weren't* stakeholders in the business.

The CEO had a unique view of people, sure, but also an outdated one. When he said people were at the center of the business, he meant people across the business existed to drive financial results for their shareholders. This mentality isn't necessarily wrong—just myopic and incomplete. It was driven by economist and Nobel laureate Milton Friedman's 1970 article published in the *New York Times* titled "A Friedman Doctrine—The Social Responsibility of Business Is to Increase Its Profits," and commonly known as the Friedman doctrine or *shareholder theory*, which has been a core component of American business thinking for decades.

As you might've guessed by now, it's also a quickly crumbling pillar in the Old Work Exchange. Signaling a new era, a 2021 article published by the University of Chicago (which was Friedman's academic institution as a professor) was titled "Is the Friedman Doctrine Still Relevant in the 21st Century?"

The article, published almost exactly fifty years after Friedman's famous doctrine, marked a change happening across the business world. The article's author, Amy Merrick, wrote, "Contemporary businesses are navigating a fraught landscape in which many of them are being called upon to declare their priorities. Companies in every industry must decide to whom they are responsible, and for what—

and if they choose to look beyond shareholder value in determining their agenda, what that means in practice."[38]

With all that in mind, let's go back to my former employer with its "very unique" culture. Shareholder value drove everything— employees were a means to a profitable end. There were no stakeholders across the organization itself—shareholders were the only stakeholders. That is, the company operated with shareholder primacy.

The company had firmly decided to whom it was responsible, but it liked to put a spin on workers operating the business by saying people were at the core of the business. Again, optics and messaging aren't enough. Empty statements don't cut it in the New Work Exchange.

The future of work isn't shareholder theory as espoused by Friedman, but *stakeholder theory*, carefully detailed in R. Edward Freeman's 1984 seminal book *Strategic Management: A Stakeholder Approach*. All those decades ago, Freeman wrote: "Somewhere in the past, organizations were quite simple, and 'doing business' consisted of buying raw materials from suppliers, converting it to products, and selling it to customers ... We are in need of new concepts ... which reorient our way of looking at the world to encompass present and future changes."[39] At the core of Freeman's argument was that organizations create relationships with stakeholders that guide and inform organizational strategy. Businesses that follow this approach create a stakeholder ecosystem for delivering value.

So what is a stakeholder exactly? A stakeholder is "a party that has an interest in a company and can either affect or be affected by the business."[40] Why did I end up leaving the company with the obnoxious CEO? There were many reasons, but a central reason was that their leadership wanted the company to remain comfortably in the status quo, operating with "employees" and a mindset of "we and they." If the idea is that workers keep the cogs at the center of a business moving, that paradigm leaves little room for people to be a true part of the business. If workers aren't people, they're certainly not stakeholders.

Yet people are the most important stakeholders in every business—whether the business acknowledges this or not.

> People are the most important stakeholders in every business— whether the business acknowledges this or not.

Despite all the pandemic-related aspects that have changed work, the reality is that work was already changing decades ago, as Freeman's philosophy shows. It's shifting toward people—a shift that can give companies a unique and competitive advantage. Remember, there are stages of change. Embracing the shift toward people and stakeholders is far more effective if we proactively work to create change instead of reactively waiting for the change to happen magically.

Some of the most influential voices in business have been pushing for this approach in recent years. In 2019, Business Roundtable announced a new "Statement of Purpose of a Corporation" that was signed by 181 CEOs, all of whom committed to leading "for the benefit of all stakeholders—customers, employees, suppliers, communities, and shareholders." As part of the statement, Tricia Griffith, the president and CEO of Progressive Corporation is quoted as saying: "CEOs work to generate profits and return value to shareholders, but the best-run companies do more. They put the customer first and invest in their employees and communities. In the end, it's the most promising way to build long-term value."[41]

We've begun to pivot away from shareholder primary and toward stakeholders—however, there's still a lot of work to do as part of that shift. Over the past years, several manufacturing, processing, and distilling companies have ended up in the media because they refused to allow their production-line workers enough time to take bathroom breaks. Employees resorted to wearing adult diapers at work to prevent getting written up for taking too long in the bathroom.

Every time these stories unfold, I feel a great sense of urgency to do what I can to promote alternatives. We should all be wondering how these types of issues can *still* be happening at work! They'll continue until our mindset and practices abandon the shareholder-first mindset. It's time to run *away from* not aligning to stakeholder-ship and *toward* being a stakeholder.

That's exactly what I did, by the way. While we don't always follow our own advice, that time I did. No regrets, either.

DEFINING INTERNAL AND EXTERNAL STAKEHOLDERS

In the past, the term "stakeholders" was often used interchangeably with "shareholders." Occasionally the definition extended to other professional business partnerships that organizations viewed as critical to financial success. The term was often associated with financial capital—that is, where the *money*, the literal capital, comes from—not human capital.

Let's redefine it. Stakeholders are *anyone with an interest in an organization's success*—specifically defining "success" as more than stock performance or return on investment. Or, said another way, it's someone who cares about an organization and adopts a sense of ownership in the success of the organization.

If a person is an active steward for an organization's mission, goals, outlook, brand, process, people, or vision, then that person is a stakeholder. That can include employees, customers, vendors, and government institutions. While shareholders are *types* of stakeholders, they aren't by any means the *only* stakeholders. The results of ignoring stakeholders aren't positive. As Dr. Freeman once stated in an interview, "A company can't ignore any of its stakeholders and truly succeed."[42]

The New Work Exchange understands that people who work within organizations are *the first group* of stakeholders to be considered. As their success drives organizational success—including shareholder success—we should understand that "employees" are *primary* stakeholders in every business.

> **Are all stakeholders created equal? Wrong question. Instead, we must ask how we can engage all stakeholders to have the maximum possible impact on our businesses.**

The way I look at it, there are two sets of stakeholders: internal and external.

Internal stakeholders are the people working *inside* a business, such as the owners and employees, because they're directly impacted by what's happening at the company. While external stakeholders have an interest in the success of the business, they're not directly impacted by the work itself. These could include customers, shareholders, suppliers, vendors, government institutions, community institutions, and the media.

Are all stakeholders created equal? Wrong question. Instead, we must ask how we can engage all stakeholders to have the maximum possible impact on our businesses. Employees are and always will be our most important stakeholders. Full stop. Customers and investors follow—in that order. The key isn't to strive to deliver what each group individually desires but to seek, find, and deliver for the collective. Look for wins that serve the needs across all stakeholders.

Seeing people as primary stakeholders isn't an either-or choice. The only way to engage people is to make it known they are important to their organizations. From an employee's perspective, this shift in thinking can make the difference between just "having a job" or showing up to work because they want to be an integral part of an organization. It's a clearly drawn line that distinguishes those who feel invested from those who don't.

Stakeholdership prevents the "caring problem" I mentioned earlier in this book. Magic happens among those who see themselves as organizational stewards. Workplaces are most often transformed by stewards and stakeholders. Perhaps that's why so many employee-owned companies are renowned for their success—both with customers *and* employees. Some of the best-known and most successful employee-owned companies: Publix Super Markets, WinCo Foods, and W. L. Gore & Associates.[43]

Besides, CEOs are no longer only accountable to a board of directors and shareholders. They're also accountable to their employees, customers, social media, and social causes. In March of 2022, headlines blew up with the story of Vishal Garg, CEO of Better.com, firing nine hundred employees over a Zoom call. Leaked emails revealed how he'd previously called employees "dumb dolphins" and reprimanded them by claiming, "YOU ARE EMBARRASSING ME."[44] Yes, he used all caps just like that.

Obviously, this did incredible damage to the reputation of the company, not to mention Garg. His frustration stemmed from low projections that would need to be reported to investors. This tells me he was operating on the belief that shareholders are first and people second ... or, based on his leaked emails, maybe even lower. Such an approach only breeds organizational dysfunction and sabotages long-term success.

The New Work Exchange requires us to retire this belief system and reset our relationships with people. The most effective and profitable organizations in the world understand the roles employees—*people*—play in their success. Those organizations work diligently to protect and leverage that relationship for the benefit of all.

RETHINKING HUMAN CAPITAL

A lot of my ideas come across as top-line thinking, so let's shift to a bottom-line perspective for a moment. There are many ways to grow a business, but all of them require investment in some form of capital. Various types of capital help produce value or gain an advantage in the marketplace. When an organization wants to achieve something, it must rely on capital to make it happen. While there are several different types of capital (social, natural, political), the two most critical are financial and human.

Let's get financial capital out of the way first. It's almost always associated with anything that has monetary value and can be used toward creating future value and growth. This is true, whether you're building a business or budgeting for groceries. Money isn't the only way to get things done, but it can do a lot, and you probably don't really need (or want) me to give you a lecture about it. Going back to *shareholder theory* for a moment: When financial capital is made *ultimate*, shareholders are placed above everything (and everyone) else.

Human capital, on the other hand, consists of the collective skills, expertise, capabilities, health, and practical know-how within and among the people who work within an organization. Unlike other types of capital, human capital is virtually unlimited, which confers on it an incredibly important and unique rationale for all forms of investment, including financial capital.

Tapping into human capital is about more than just living up to slogans like "Put People First" or "People Are Our Greatest Asset." It's about investing time and resources into the best areas to propel growth in people. As an association that specializes in Total Rewards, Worldat-Work has been informing financial decisions on human capital for more than sixty-five years. Rewards and human capital are inextricably linked. This lens provides a way of rethinking our employment relationships—from full-time employees to gig workers, part-time folks, and consultants. It's time to think about how to invest in people across the organization.

> **Human capital is virtually unlimited, which confers on it an incredibly important and unique rationale for all forms of investment, including financial capital.**

In other words, it's not enough to just send people off to a conference once a year or set aside $1,500 for employees to have access to during the year to grow their skills. That's already an old-school way of thinking. Learning must become part of the work experience, absorbed into every aspect of organizations.

How are you preparing team members for the next stages in their careers or lives? Failing to do so means vital team members are treated like cogs in the machine, not true stakeholders.

One of the strongest models I've seen for fostering growth is building an internship program within a company. I'm not talking about bringing in young people to work for free or low pay like a typical internship model—I'm talking about internships to invest in the people already within an organization. By exposing people to new roles and departments, skills are increased (upskilling), and new skills are learned (reskilling). What if 10 percent of a person's time was spent getting cross-trained or retrained to double their skills? That's a very smart human capital investment.

The apprenticeship model sounds old school, but it's very applicable today. We're seeing companies create such opportunities, telling their people, "Hey, you don't need to go get a degree for this. We'll put you through a six-month course so you can be successful in learning whatever new skills you're seeking." We need more innovative thinking like that because, frankly, most companies are behind in their skill sets and not doing enough to invest in the skills needed for the success of their human capital.

INVESTING IN HUMAN CAPITAL

Should employees always have been stakeholders? Yes, but the effects of *not* treating employees as stakeholders weren't always as obvious, which is why shareholders have dominated corporate thinking and strategy for so long. Shareholders tend to do very little except demand more from organizations—more to hit numbers, more squeezed from margins, and so on. When that's contrasted with employees as your stakeholders, then we recognize that nothing much happens without them. That fact alone should drive our desire to create value for our people—they are the true value generators in our businesses.

Where do we start investing in our people? How do we increase our investment in human capital and ultimately engage people as stakeholders? Let's look at a few places to start.

DECLARING STAKEHOLDERSHIP

This one is so simple. Determine who your stakeholders are, and detail the definition. Include differentiation for internal and external stakeholders as well as primary and secondary levels. Then make the definition public. Show people they're stakeholders, where they fit in, and why they are so important to the ecosystem, results, and future of your business. Don't forget to include vendors, community members, and even employees' families when possible.

While actions speak louder than words, sometimes we need to start with words as these steps provide context. Putting anything and everything on paper is a great accountability measure—both to hold organizations accountable in decision-making and to guide alignment to the stakeholder list.

Furthermore, it reinforces why and how stakeholders are accountable for organizational success.

One of our core values at WorldatWork is "Own the Outcome." It's our way of communicating to people that we all have ownership over work. With this value, we're stating that we trust our people. If it's an unwritten rule in an organization that employees are the primary stakeholders, that's a way to make it explicit.

DEMONSTRATING HOW PEOPLE ARE IMPORTANT

Saying people are important must be followed by *making* people important. It turns out the old adage "Actions speak louder than words" is still true. A solid strategy for Total Rewards goes a long way in helping people feel secure and connected. In many ways, it takes a layer of worry away from day-to-day life so people can focus on bigger things. But that alone isn't enough.

Look for ways to demonstrate to primary stakeholders you have their backs. A basic example: When a customer is very upset, back the employee while calming the customer—even if the employee was wrong. In other words, it's time to ditch phrases like "The customer is always right" because frankly, that's bogus and irresponsible. Customers are wrong all the time—they just can't be made to feel that way.

While both employees and customers are stakeholders, team members must be primary stakeholders. Never let customer focus be so extreme that we damage our relationships with our people. There's sufficient room for both stakeholder groups to win, be heard, and help grow our businesses.

One of the ways to gauge how well we're doing in this regard is by looking at where money gets spent. Quantify and qualify to demonstrate how much investment is going toward people. If the numbers show limited investment is going toward our greatest asset—people—then it creates a basis for adjustments.

In the New Work Exchange, we need to prove what we say. Our core values are tested all the time. When they become inconvenient, do we still uphold them? Do we pass the infamous stress test? It might be more difficult to do the right thing, but when core stakeholders—people—are involved, are we willing to take risks and stand by what we've claimed to value? Nothing is definitively important until we're authentic and genuine about it.

The bad news with this? Employees get it first. The great news? Employees get it first.

As you might expect, considering my experience talking with (but not being allowed to interview) Donna, one of my favorite ways to engage a team is to involve people in hiring new team members— including new bosses. The sense of ownership, importance, and confidence people get when they get to have a say in who's hired and who leads them reinforces authentic stakeholdership.

KNOWING ME BEFORE YOU NEED ME

If people only come to see you when there's a problem, well, that's a problem. To become more approachable, you need to approach others first—and not just with a new assignment or problem. During an interview I did at a WorldatWork event with Judy Shepard of the Matthew Shepard Foundation, she imparted a powerful approach to improving work that's stayed with me: be sure that "you know me before you need me." How wise! All too often, we assume that we have the necessary relationships to get things done. Titles and roles only go so far.

Open, ongoing, and meaningful dialogue initiated from the very beginning goes a long way. An "open door policy" doesn't mean much if no one feels the freedom to walk *through* the open door. Working from home has also completely removed the door from the equation. It's now so difficult to have chance meetings in hallways, which often lead to great conversations.

At the beginning of the last chapter, I told a story in which I felt frustrated after joining an organization experiencing significant issues and how my focus on the business prevented me from focusing on the people around me. A tactical error I made in that scenario was expecting others to first engage me.

Without first establishing that it was OK to discuss *anything*— cats, kids, sporting events, the newest superhero movie, or an under-performing colleague—I'd expected to get down to business without first facing the people in the business. I'd not yet established relationships with anyone—no one knew my approach or motivations. I hadn't had a real dialogue with anyone, as I'd been trying to understand the business. Only when we share information as part of a dialogue can we decide *whether* and *when* to act on anything.

Dialogue may be easier for those who are extraverted, sociable, and good at small talk—for others, it can prove challenging. We must invite each other into genuine opportunities for dialogue and discussion. The more frequently we invite and provide open forums, the more comfortable people become at sharing whatever *they* decide to disclose about themselves.

Dialogue can extend beyond the walls—physical or digital—of the workplace. Recently, I was struck by the story of a company that was going through intense changes. They knew things would be very challenging for their employees. Before these changes started, the CEO sent a letter to the families of the employees, letting them know their family members would be going through a lot of stress over the next several months and to please provide them with extra care, support, and understanding if they came home tired or frustrated. Furthermore, the letter included a gift card for the family to use as needed during the changes.

When employees were asked about the impact of these letters, you could feel their deep appreciation, and their families were incredibly impressed by the CEO's transparency, consideration, and approach. That's the power of good dialogue.

DISCARDING LABELS

Since I am obsessed with making work better, I always like to learn what organizations are doing to both engage and disengage their workers. Once, I consulted at an organization that couldn't figure out why they had such high levels of disengagement. It didn't take me long to see the pattern affecting this company. My first trip to their headquarters corresponded with their annual holiday celebration. There were two massive tents behind the office. The tents were for different people—one for management and one for nonmanagement.

Really. Two tents, same company.

I was curious whether the amenities were the same. They weren't. While the intention may have been to tell managers they were important and appreciated, I worried about other messages this approach communicated. What did this say to nonmanagers? What did it reinforce for managers? Implicit messages exist in almost every organizational action and decision.

In the quest to set people up for success, we tend to label things. When you think of job descriptions, it's right there on the page—the title of the job and the data about the function of the job. Sometimes in our quest for efficiency, we're guilty of forgetting what these labels might communicate to people.

A common job title and classification over the past century has been "unskilled hourly worker." Originally, this approach was designed to clarify whether a job required a specific technical skill or whether the job could be completed without prior training. It's common to think of this as a carryover term from the days of heavy manufacturing, but that isn't the case.

When Eric Adams became the mayor of New York City, he pushed for organizations to bring their employees back to the office after the pandemic. While not intentional, he perpetuated the "unskilled and skilled" dynamic when he said: "My low-skill workers—my cooks, my dishwashers, my messengers, my shoeshine people, those that work in Dunkin' Donuts—they don't have the academic skills to sit in the corner office. They need this."[45]

People who perform these roles aren't "unskilled" or "low skilled." There are many reasons these roles were deemed "essential" during the pandemic. Some people perform repetitive tasks as part of their role, but that doesn't make them unskilled. They simply have different skills, which can be said about any of us!

This *skilled-versus-unskilled* approach to titles leads to a more siloed and stratified organization. It's time we retire this classification, which signals and labels differences in *value*. Further, it's misleading and inaccurate—and might explain why we have such significant skill gaps. If half of your workforce is considered unskilled labor, you are going to have a lot of work to do to ensure they feel like true stakeholders.

Consider this: If my manager thinks I'm unskilled, is there any incentive to grow my skills? Is there a path to go from unskilled to skilled? You may not use this title, but many of our customers, service providers, and governmental agencies do. According to the US Bureau of Labor Statistics, these "unskilled" jobs represent most jobs in the United States.[46]

Even accepted workplace phrases like "being on the front line" or "chain of command" can be problematic. They're war terms! Do we really want to compare work and war? Such labels and phrases send the wrong message.

We can find terms and phrases that better communicate value— labels that are people centric rather than function centric. For example, "customer facing" is much more descriptive and accurate than "front line." Work is a massive part of our existence, so the labels we use have power—power to either elevate or power to reinforce inequity.

Significant validation is derived from what we do, so this is an area where we need significant alignment between people and organizations. Few people would experience long-term engagement with an organization that describes them as "on the front lines." Frontline battles and fighting in trenches were notoriously perilous. People stationed "at the front," otherwise known as the vanguard, were positioned to gain ground and position—at *any* cost. Again, is that the message we should be sharing with our people?

To go to another extreme, what if organizations decided to make everyone vice presidents? What would we lose by bringing people *up* as a strategy to level the playing field? When I was at Gore, I had a coworker who, when asked by external people about his job, always answered "There's the CEO, then me." Since Gore is a flat organization, this answer wasn't wrong. Because most organizations are still so hierarchical, it was always interesting to see people's reactions to his statement.

All of this comes down to an organization's fundamental positioning. Are we going to focus on fostering the full potential of our people? If the answer is yes, labels are a tool to elevate experiences. It's one more way to demonstrate how people count.

> Making work better isn't just a warm and fuzzy thing to do. Impact capitalism—business that maximizes impact while maximizing return—is vital to putting people first.

BECOMING AN IMPACT CAPITALIST

Making work better isn't just a warm and fuzzy thing to do. Impact capitalism—business that maximizes impact while maximizing return—is vital to putting people first. It's difficult to have alignment across an organization if what people prioritize and care about is negatively affected by things occurring *at work*. Profit isn't incompatible with migrating away from being a traditional capitalist and toward the idea of putting people first. Instead, it recognizes that when people come first, profits *do follow*.

We don't have to pick one or the other—we can make money *and* have an impact. Doing so means that time and resources are dedicated to helping people connect with value and purpose. It's integral for people to have a *why* for work. At the same time, companies have their own *why*. Knowing why we're working keeps us focused, dedicated, and engaged—even at the most challenging moments.

It's possible to focus on our individual and organizational *why* without sacrificing profits along the way. When we're impact focused, it translates into a positive experience for internal and external stakeholders, which generates more sustainable profit.

A great example I've seen of impact capitalism was a company that, as part of their new-hire orientation, had a team-building exercise during which new hires built a dollhouse together. When it was completed, they delivered the dollhouse to a family in need. This not only made an impact on a child in their community but also made an impact on the new hires, injecting meaning and goodwill into their work as they got to know each other.

COACHING AND FIRING BAD BOSSES

In the New Work Exchange, there's no room for bad bosses. They were expensive before the pandemic, but the cost is escalating. Remember when we looked at the *state of work* at the beginning of this book? The numbers weren't great. To frame the data we review, let's focus on an insight from the book *First, Break All the Rules: What the World's Greatest Managers Do Differently*: "People leave managers, not companies."[47] Showing this claim hasn't lost its relevance, a 2022 study by GoodHire showed that 82 percent of American workers said they would potentially quit their job because of a bad manager.[48]

In 2018, *Harvard Business Review* (*HBR*) also unpacked the idea that people quit their bosses. Even prepandemic, they concluded that when people *stay* in a role, it's because 31 percent of people found work more enjoyable, 33 percent used their strengths more often, and 37 percent gained the skills and experiences they needed to develop their careers.

What did *HBR* think this data meant? "Three key ways that managers can customize experiences for their people: enable them to do work they enjoy, help them play to their strengths, and carve a path for career development that accommodates personal priorities."[49]

Guess who doesn't do those things? A bad boss. Bad bosses rarely position team members as stakeholders.

People decide to engage or quit based on lower thresholds of a manager's behavior. A lot of factors go into defining a bad boss, but at its very core, it's about how a manager relates to those they manage. What are the chances everyone is aligned with their ideal boss? Some people just don't work well together, or they have style differences, but there's nothing more frustrating than having a terrible supervisor.

Take this moment to assess what success looks like in the context of your organization and where it is going. If you have managers with excessive turnover or poor results, take action. If you are a manager with a lot of turnover or poor results, it's time to assess why. If you aren't a manager yet but you want to be one, look for opportunities to grow a good foundation for leading.

We must also contend with opportunities to challenge hierarchy. We shouldn't reinforce limits on who can or should lead people. As organizations flatten to increase speed, teams will become more fluid, which enables talent to influence and lead across an organization.

Workplaces—and the people in them—suffer when we allow someone who's ineffective to continue to be ineffective. Is it too inconvenient to remove a team member who's ineffective? Or is it more ineffective to perpetuate their results? Furthermore, managers who lead through fear-based tactics are carryovers from a different age. People must be coached to realize that trust is a commodity that pays off way more than fear. High expectations don't require a trail of destruction. It's natural to want to say, "Because I said so; that's why." But when I find myself wanting to say it, I take a mini-time-out to refocus on the longer wins.

The quality of our work relationships impacts everything we do, from top-line growth to the bottom line, from customer engagement to employee engagement and retention. Bad managers are costly to our organizations—they ultimately create bad workplaces and hinder company performance.

EMPOWERING LOCAL DECISION-MAKING

I've said this before, but it's too important to stakeholdership not to repeat. People must be empowered to make decisions. At a recent WorldatWork event, I got to interview Coca-Cola's chief HR officer, Lisa Chang. The organization has more than seven hundred thousand employees, so I asked her, "How do you get people aligned at Coke to get done all of the amazing things you do?"

"It's really all about guidelines," Lisa answered. "There's no way we can have a policy that covers every scenario. We're big; things are very dynamic. We want to put good thinking in front of people through guidelines and allow them to make a good decision. For Coca-Cola, it is about giving as much choice as we can."

That choice serves Coca-Cola well. Founded in 1892, Coca-Cola products are sold in two hundred countries across the globe. In 2021, LinkedIn rated the company a top employer in Atlanta, Georgia,[50] and in 2022, Coca-Cola's Europacific Partners New Zealand was named an employer of choice for a fourth year in a row by HRD's Employer of Choice Awards.[51]

By being flexible with guidelines rather than strict policies, they created a more flexible workplace. People felt more supported. Because control was put in the hands of local teams and people, speed and efficiency increased. This sentiment is reflected in other aspects of Coca-Cola's operation and culture as well. In a 2021 interview about the employee experience, Coca-Cola's Bottling Investments Group's Global Chief People Officer Drew Fernandez said, "[Driving] utmost simplification across all of our people offerings ... has been a big theme for Coca-Cola—we really want to make sure that we simplify our processes and approach ... Sometimes in the complexity, this is where you miss the mark—and sometimes incur additional, unnecessary expenses. If you're able to drive simplicity, you're able to create cost efficiencies, but also elevate the employee experience."[52]

Not only should decision-making be decentralized from a corporate perspective whenever possible, but good leaders also must do it on a local level by empowering the people they supervise to make their own decisions instead of needing approval on every item. That's really the foundation of stakeholdership.

When leaders adopt more of a mentoring mindset instead of just pushing out orders, it empowers people.

For one thing, things speed up with this approach, which we'll talk about in the next chapter.

More importantly, it increases the experience of trust and ownership. When leaders adopt more of a mentoring mindset instead of just pushing out orders, it empowers people. Being available to provide insight and direction with the more difficult issues which arise facilitates better decision-making the next time around.

In other words: Get out of everyone's way! Doing so will also get you out of your own way. When people are hired to be stakeholders, and that mentality is reinforced over time, we've got to remember those people are in place *to guide business decisions*, not the other way around!

REWARDING AND SHARING COLLECTIVELY

When Sara Blakely, the founder and CEO of Spanx, announced her company's acquisition deal, she followed it up with an announcement that she was giving every employee $10,000 and two first-class plane tickets. Recognizing—and rewarding—her people, she declared everyone as a stakeholder. "This is a very big moment for each and every one of you," Blakely announced.[53] *That's* recognizing stakeholders and their contributions!

Being generous and rewarding people means more than just giving people more money, though. You can be generous with recognition, flexibility, understanding, and ways for them to get involved in issues they care about. The most effective rewards communicate and reinforce *how people are valued stakeholders*. If a reward encourages a person to be the best they can be, it's meaningful and gives you a lot to build off for continued engagement.

CALLING ALL STAKEHOLDERS

Profitability, success, impact, and growth don't have to be mutually exclusive. Establishing stakeholders across our organizations really changes *how we do business*, not the results we're seeking. We have an opportunity to replace obsolete processes and costly policies that slow things down with new practices that allow people *and* businesses to flourish together.

This is the prime moment to achieve a new way to work—specifically, a new way to work *with* others in a meaningful, collective manner toward a shared mission. Remember, though, we aren't only welcoming in more stakeholders; we're also saying goodbye to the Old Work Exchange. This has been foreshadowed by many signals—like the elimination of guaranteed pensions and expectations that employers take care of people for life. But what's replaced these perks? The New Work Exchange gives us permission to reset, rethink, and revitalize work into something much more meaningful for all of us.

The New Work Exchange fosters stronger connections and alignment between organizations and people. It frees up—rather than limits—organizations to seek out new wins for each stakeholder. The reality is that work isn't about "us" and "them." It's always been about "us."

CHAPTER 6

Finding Our Pace in a Much Faster World

The world is *faster than ever.* So work is too. But have we found our pace yet? Probably not. Here's why: the New Work Exchange will only accelerate the flow of work, *and* there's a lot of extraneous change impacting us already. Remember those stages of change I mentioned earlier? We work through things, we fall backward onto old behaviors, we learn from them, and then after developing some new muscle memory from new patterns, we're propelled forward.

The world's work is happening at a rate that seems faster than ever. How do we gain momentum and velocity in the New Work Exchange?

We understand how we got here. We learn from the past—the Old Work Exchange—and we make strategic changes to *how* and *why* we work. Then we set a new pace.

One of the most obvious factors disrupting traditional ideas of work has been the advent of faster communication, enabled through technology and higher informational bandwidth. It's made business more efficient and opened new channels of distribution—but it's also quickened the pace of business.

The culture, logistics, and fundamental ideas of leadership have been shifted in ways that have left many organizations and people struggling to catch their breath. The final step in the new era of work is finding the right pace in a world that expects everything on demand and for everyone to work faster.

Had I been born one hundred and some years earlier, my first job might not have been in fast food. Maybe it could've been with the Pony Express. From April 3, 1860, to October 26, 1861, the Pony Express operated as an express-mail service. Riders sometimes as young as fourteen years would mount their ponies in St. Joseph, Missouri, and ride through the literal wild, wild West to Sacramento, California, delivering mail at a record pace. Ten days—something many believed impossible to accomplish. It's said that in the eighteen months the service existed, only one bag of mail was ever lost.

Despite its innovation and speed, as well as its overall delivery success, the service was a financial flop and went bankrupt. One factor for the Pony Express's failure was the lack of protective infrastructure for the mail stations along the routes. While the riders themselves faced danger, only six of the six thousand riders died in the line of duty.

Meanwhile, station hands—let's imagine them as middle managers—lived in crude outposts susceptible to attacks. At least sixteen station hands were killed in the summer of 1860, early in the life of the service, which spurred on the Pyramid Lake War. The result? A temporary shutdown in service, which cost the company $75,000 and prevented the company from landing a lucrative government contract it desperately needed to survive these setbacks.[54]

Sound familiar? We know we need to work and produce faster, but velocity and momentum are difficult to establish on so many fronts, especially all at once. In our current world, speed is everything and is the new differentiator in business. But as the Pony Express should teach us, speed is only profitable if we have proper structures in place to manage and take advantage of it. The ways in which we can connect, share information, and decentralize our communication are all expanding at an unprecedented pace. However, many of our current organizational structures are inherited and obsolete and serve as speed bumps in our way.

Don't worry; this isn't about to turn into a book on Agile product development. But I do want to bring things full circle, help us propel forward, and successfully cross over into the New Work Exchange. That requires us to look critically at what's slowing us down. Across the board, there's a common thread to answer this question: communication. It's more facilitated than ever, but it's also more complex and can go off the rails much more quickly than at any other time in history.

REFLECTING: COMMUNICATION IMPLIES UNDERSTANDING

Speed is relative to our expectations. If you go to a middle school track meet, you're not expecting anyone to break any world records. If your memory and work experience travels back even fifteen years, we once considered dial-up internet fast. It was certainly faster than getting in your car, driving to the library, and spending time looking something up in a hard-copy resource. Simply posing a question to "Ask Jeeves" saved a lot of time and did *make things faster*.

Likewise, the methods in which we communicate carry their own expectations of how they are to be used. Hieroglyphics and papyrus were cutting-edge forms of communication in ancient Egypt, but they had distinct purposes. Hieroglyphics were intended to preserve information for generations. Papyrus was intended to easily carry a message but not necessarily preserve it. Skip ahead, and the Gutenberg press sought to do both—and with the speed and consistency to get material into the hands of more people at a lower cost.

We have more devices and platforms for communication than ever before, which means disconnects between us are bridged more easily (if we can afford it all). Each platform for communication carries its own expectations. For example, even if we understand that a celebrity or politician writing on a platform like Twitter is communicating their message to millions of people at once, it can somehow feel more personal and personally directed than a television address read from a teleprompter.

Changes in work practice reflect this too. How many video calls have you participated in *from your home?* When doing so, was your home not your workplace at that moment? When the pandemic hit, I was scheduled to do a live interview with actress Brooke Shields, but then it became a video call. For all intents and purposes, I invited Brooke Shields "into my home." She invited me—and all attendees at the meeting—into her home. That's quite a talking point.

Guess what? *That's the New Work Exchange*, and that's an example of setting a new work pace.

With all this advancement in how we can communicate, we also have more opportunity in the ways we can *miscommunicate*. How much work have you done over messenger apps and email over the past several years? How many times has it gone wrong or led to misinterpretation?

We see this all the time on social media, where it's difficult to interpret sarcasm. We used to have face-to-face conversations in an office, during which a million microexpressions could be incorporated and deciphered. We're tainted by those experiences and their different rules. Having a meeting at home still means we're "at work," but if the proper expectations and rules guidelines aren't set, it can quickly turn into way more than anyone bargained for. There's a big difference between information sharing and actual communication. With all these tools, there's a ton of information flying around us all day long—however, *communication* implies we *understand* each other.

When I started at WorldatWork, I implemented what Alpine Investors coined "the 100/100 rule," but my application was meant specifically for successful communication. According to Graham Weaver, a founder of Alpine, the rule was meant for "[situations] in which we commit to expend 100 percent (or more) of the work in order to come as close as possible to guaranteeing a 100 percent chance of success."[55]

When applied to communication, I tweaked this to mean that when I talk, I'm 100 percent responsible for making sure you understand what I'm saying. And when you talk, I'm also 100 percent responsible for making sure I understand what you're saying to me.

In other words, we want to avoid hearing things like "Well, you didn't explain that" or "That's not how I understood it." If you truly don't understand what is being said, it's your job to ask for clarity: "Joe, it sounds like you're saying this. Am I understanding that right?" And if you're not understanding it right, it gives Joe the opportunity to rephrase things until everyone understands. You still may not agree, but at least you'll be further along on understanding each other.

Remember, alignment is everything. With so much rushing, a lack of alignment of any kind prevents and undermines real momentum and speed.

Who hasn't been upset by something a colleague said over email? We used to have a person on our sales team who made work-related irritation very clear. Responses would be sent in email. In all caps. Real annoyance was demonstrated with words in red text. We've all experienced something similar.

With the speed at which we're exchanging information, there *ISN'T* (caps just for fun) always going to be the opportunity to hash things out in old-school ways. We aren't always going to huddle in a room together, be able to read one another's tone and body language, or have a casual chat in the hallway. And unfortunately, we're seeing our communication styles being *affected and trained* by the tech itself.

For example, you might see someone being sharp and pointed in their responses because that's how tweets have conditioned our communication. These tools give us more voice, but sometimes *more voice* leads us outside the boundaries of the traditional workplace. I've heard leaders say, "Get this information down to the essentials. Give me the tweet." The same people have then changed their mind and said they need more context and detail after receiving the tweet version they asked for. We still need to do what it takes to listen, absorb, and understand—and wherever possible, be flexible *and* consistent. It's a tall order.

What I like about the 100/100 rule for communication is that it lays out a consistent expectation, regardless of the medium used. It puts communication first and technology second—because technology is going to change, and who knows what it'll look like ten years from now? Whatever tools we're using to quickly communicate as a team, it's a timeless principle that can guide us toward meaningful communication rather than just information sharing.

PUTTING PEOPLE OVER PLATFORM AND PROCESS

Having good expectations around communication will still only get us so far. We can apply the 100/100 rule, the best tech tools available, *and* a tech-savvy staff but still run into communication problems. How so?

All too often we put processes over people rather than people over processes.

Technology can help us decentralize our work and decision-making. It can also connect us with the people who have the right answers.

> **All too often we put processes over people rather than people over processes.**

But if we have outdated processes or platforms in place, it's actually more difficult for people to get work done in a timely fashion. In many ways, we're using twenty-first-century technology within nineteenth-century expectations. It's a problem if systems get in the team's way instead of facilitating speed, usability, and usefulness.

For example, let's say you're a salesperson preparing for a presentation with a dream client. You're getting your materials together and double-checking the slides and then realize the demo video in the presentation is several years old. Didn't you hear a new one had been put together by the marketing team?

There are a couple of scenarios for what could happen next that I want to run by you. Which one will serve you better?

ASSESSING SCENARIO 1

Let's say your company has a structure in place that frowns upon cross-departmental communication. It's viewed as too chaotic, so there's long been an expectation that you must run all requests regarding changes in the sales presentation by your supervisor first. So you message your supervisor:

"I have the big presentation with Dream Client tomorrow. Can I update the demo video with the new one marketing has been developing?"

"I'm not sure," they reply. "I need to run this by the sales VP first and make sure it's OK for you to use this video. I don't know if it's been fully vetted yet."

You wait for thirty minutes … do some work … sixty minutes … make a couple of calls. The clock is ticking toward the end of the day. You message your supervisor again.

"Hey, any word on the new demo video?"

A few more minutes pass by and then, "The video is ready, but he hasn't received approval from the CEO to start using it yet, and she's traveling."

ASSESSING SCENARIO 2

Speed is of the essence, and your company trusts you know how to do your job the best, so you directly message the video lead on the marketing team and ask, "Hey, is the new demo video complete? If so, can you tell me where to find it?"

And then perhaps your colleague in marketing responds a few minutes later, "Sure, here it is attached. Good luck!" Or else, "Sorry, it's not finished yet and is still being reviewed. The old one you have is the best we've got for now. Good luck!"

You get the picture?

Technology can solve some of our communication problems, but it also has the power to help us decentralize decision-making so we can work better and faster—as long as we work to remove the obsolete structures standing in the way. One change we can all make immediately—individually and organizationally—is to level our approach to communication. Go to the *person* who has the answer to the question, not the title. Nothing squashes innovation and ideas like a strict hierarchy.

If I encountered the first scenario at a company, my first question would be, "Why does the CEO have to give approval on the sales demo video? Does she regularly sit in on sales meetings with clients?" Chances are the answer will be, "Not in a long time," or worse, "She's never been in a sales role a day in her life." In the New Work Exchange, we need to remove constraints continuously and help people take on more decision-making. Yes, mistakes can occur in the short term, but there'll be more growth and effectiveness in the long term.

This scenario, rather than being an entertaining piece of fiction, is still the reality many people face—an egregious bureaucratic structure failing to keep pace with today's speed of business. Too often, leaders groan about needing to find ways to boost productivity without realizing the processes they've created are working against them. It's the Disney example all over again, where well-intentioned processes complicated communication for the creative team, undermining their ability to succeed.

Decisions that must travel up and down the corporate ladder at a snail's pace are relics of a bygone era. We've got to go directly to the person (not necessarily the title) with the answer to the question so things can move quickly. One of the reasons things moved so quickly when I was at Gore was because there was no formal hierarchy preventing communication. Flatter communication moved faster and with more fluidity. Everyone could go directly to the person who could help, which avoided multiple people in a chain of command.

We live in a culture of instant gratification. Nobody is satisfied with the status quo. We know what we want, and we want it now! And guess what? That doesn't have to be a bad thing.

When you're hungry and pull into a drive-through, you don't want to wait an hour for your food because the expectation is that a "fast-food" restaurant will bring you some food fast. If you spot a mistake on your paycheck that doubled the amount taken out of your check, you don't want to hear, "It's going to take finance a month to get this sorted out." You want to hear, "Sorry, let me fix that for you now."

We've all been a frustrated customer at some point and asked the person on the other end of the phone, "Can I speak to your manager?" That's because we've been conditioned to hierarchical workplaces. Too often we assume the first person we engage with in customer support is an entry-level employee who is unable to resolve challenges. We've learned to make these assumptions *because* hierarchical organizations too often *don't* empower customer-facing team members.

Again, there are no unskilled workers in the New Work Exchange. Problem-solving power needs to be in the hands of customer-facing people. This not only creates happier customers—but it also creates happier team members, empowered by a greater sense of ownership and enabled to make a difference with customers.

The outdated response "Let me talk to my manager about this" has launched millions of memes for a reason. This approach tells the customer, "Hey, I've got to go through some bureaucratic red tape before I can meet your needs." This creates a missed opportunity to quickly meet a need and ultimately impacts customer loyalty as well as brand affection. Getting back to stakeholders, it also tells people they aren't valued in their organization.

Some might be afraid this strips all power from the "higher-ups" who have worked hard to earn the positions they're in. In reality, it makes absolutely no one redundant or irrelevant. Instead, it speeds things up for everyone across organizations by freeing up the ability to focus skills and talents where they truly belong. When everyone isn't putting out fires or triaging, it changes work—for the better.

> When everyone isn't putting out fires or triaging, it changes work—for the better.

STRIVING FOR MORE

Something happened in 1954 that offers us a profound and important clue for what is taking place in business today. English runner Roger Bannister accomplished a feat attempted by many other runners for decades but had eluded everyone: running a mile in less than four minutes. Until he achieved this feat, it was widely believed to be unachievable, impossible. Many thought attempts to run at such a speed for such a distance were even life-threatening.

It took decades for the mile to be run in less than four minutes, but then Bannister's record was broken forty-six days later. Seconds were shaved off Bannister's record. As time passed, more runners shaved off additional time. Moroccan runner Hicham El Guerrouj holds the current world record for the mile with a time of 3:43.13.

These accomplishments astonished the world. How did people get faster?

A critical study in 2008 attempted to answer this question. Stanford biologist Mark Denny reviewed a massive data set of records to determine whether animals had also increased their speed over time or whether there was something unique affecting human speed.[56] Denny compiled a hundred years of records and analyzed them and found that while the speed of racing horses and greyhounds had stagnated for decades, humans continued to get faster.

But why? According to Dr. Peter Weyand from Southern Methodist University, alongside technological advancements, humans have been driven to become faster by a combination of rewards—such as financial gain and status.[57] Advancements in training techniques, tools, and environments (even the optimization of running tracks themselves) have influenced human speed. Additionally, some competitions are done with the world watching—talk about a psychological impact!

All of this brings numerous implications for work today and into the future. Competition is at an all-time high in a globalized market. Mergers and acquisitions increased during and after the pandemic. Finally, the types of rewards that organizations can offer (and that people are looking for) are more diverse than at any time in recent history.

One of the many by-products of the pandemic will be the speed at which organizations can get things done. On average, developing a vaccine takes around eleven years, yet vaccinations for COVID-19 were developed in 326 days. They went through the same stage gates, protocols, and procedures as prior vaccines—it was all just done *faster* and with more support across governments and organizations. Communication, collaboration, and execution were faster because we needed them to be.

Speed isn't nice. It's necessary. It's a differentiator. This is why we see fast-food chains designing restaurants with multiple drive-through lanes and eliminating menu items that take too long to make. Curbside pickup areas were designed and constructed seemingly overnight during the pandemic, and they're here to stay. Why? Because of the speed and differentiation they offer. People are proactively implementing ways to set a new pace because the risk of being too slow is substantial.

Ways to impact performance are infinite. It all starts with the incentives, interventions, and experiences we create for our people.

Before he passed away in 2018, Roger Bannister shared the simple truth about the record he set for running the mile: "As it became clear that somebody was going to do it, I felt that I would prefer it to be me."[58] His driving force was simply the desire to be first. Our stakeholders (internal and external) also place value on being first—whether it's a response to a social issue, the hiring process, or even a new way to work.

In the spirit of Roger Bannister, if someone were to be first in reaching the New Work Exchange, wouldn't you prefer it be *you?* It's not an overstatement to say being out front has extreme economic and cultural value. In a world where start-ups pop up at intense rates, being first will remain coveted. It's imperative to leverage our abilities to create, make, and sell at warp speed.

GAINING VELOCITY AND MOMENTUM

The irony is that we may have to slow down—at first—to get faster. Again, remember those stages of change. It all takes time. The more we do it, the more velocity and momentum we develop. So start the work *now*.

ADDRESSING BOTTLENECKS

If you've determined that decisions in your organization are bottle-necked somewhere or aren't being made at the appropriate organizational level, then what needs to happen to move things? What decisions can be pushed further into the organization so stakeholders can make and receive answers on the spot?

Hotels are a great example of how this shift is playing out. Traditionally, front-desk people have been trained to do two things—check people in and out. But because they are customer-facing employees, who does a customer call when they have no hot water? They call the front desk.

In the past, the front-desk person would receive a complaint and have to get their manager on the phone. After explaining the problem, the manager would call a service person to fix the problem. But that's too slow. By then, the frustrated customer would've put their "Do Not Disturb" sign on their door and gone to bed. Before nodding off, that customer likely would have written a scathing online review.

How is this changing? Front-desk employees have been enabled to resolve any problem up to specific cost thresholds. This approach speeds up problem-solving for customers—it also increases efficiency and engagement for staff who don't have to keep calling a manager for solutions.

LOOKING FOR EXCESS

One time, I was working with a major airline and discovered their employee orientation manual was an eight-hundred-page behemoth. They'd tried to account for every possible scenario that could possibly happen. They wanted to be able to say, "That's covered on page 678—you'll find your answer in there." While this may sound thorough and technically accurate, it also misses an opportunity to help people learn not only what's *expected* but also the *meaning* behind it. As humans, we learn best by being a part of the process, not by being bystanders.

At the time, this airline would literally have new employees sit in a big room with desks to fill out their benefits paperwork while this monstrosity of a handbook was handed to them. Employees were asked to read through the manual and let someone know "if they had any questions." What a missed opportunity to engage and build strong relationships!

Since groups across the organization had contributed to the handbook, replacing pieces of it with onboarding sessions would have given people within departments opportunities to build relationships with new colleagues. Instead, it became a monster handbook written in silos across the organization, which was handed to new recruits to give them the "lay of the land."

The airline knew they needed to speed things up without jeopardizing safety in any way. As part of revising their practices across the organization, they adapted their onboarding process. A *much more condensed* sixty-five-page employee manual focused on the airline's initiative to work collaboratively to increase safety *and* delight passengers. It worked. Whether it was a cause or a correlation, they improved nearly every internal metric and ended up being on the Fortune 100 Best Places to Work list.

ADAPTING SCHEDULES

While some of the changes we need are cultural or procedural, others involve our schedules. Our on-demand culture has impacted traditional timing. Most companies have everything set up on an annual cycle—raises, performance reviews, culture surveys—and I suggest we examine whether this approach actually meets stakeholder needs.

I would argue that waiting twelve months for anything in the New Work Exchange puts us at a disadvantage. It's just much too slow for where we are and what we need. And ironically, we've set that pace *for ourselves*.

Let's look at feedback loops for team members and performance reviews. Speed is the new differentiator in all aspects of work. Should we be waiting a year to tell someone where we need them to grow, evolve, and bridge gaps?

On the flip side, if an employee has had a negative experience, then do we want them to wait for the next annual culture survey to share information about what they experienced? Waiting so long prevents fixing the problem, which risks extreme damage—to team members, customers, and the organization. In other words, solve problems while they're still small.

> **Waiting so long prevents fixing the problem, which risks extreme damage—to team members, customers, and the organization. In other words, solve problems while they're still small.**

Make a list of every annual process you currently have in place, and assess whether that pace is truly sufficient to meet your team's needs. Do the same with any calendarized and scheduled processes or deliverables. Chances are that you need to add in some poll surveys or some channels for anonymous feedback to set the optimal pace.

Your organization might already have net promoter scores in place for gauging customer satisfaction, but do you have the same thing for *employee satisfaction*? After all, the faster you can take control of negative experiences and fix problems, the better it'll be for everyone.

Annual employee-experience surveys are simply too slow and create too much data to process all at once, which creates the risk of missing important things. Instead, surveys to measure employee experiences daily, weekly, monthly, and in real time should be the norm.

BUILDING GO TEAMS

One of my favorite tactics is to assemble a "tiger team" or "go team" to come up with organizational solutions that address a specific problem or need. These are small teams of people—maybe three or four—who are gathered based on their skills. Sometimes organizations try this technique but can't get past assembling a team based on function or title. The thing I frequently hear is, "OK, we need a marketing person, a salesperson, and a customer service person for this team." Instead, focus on skill and ambition to solve new problems with new solutions.

For example, let's assume you're a hospital administrator and want to look at how to improve the patient experience. A title-based hospital might assign a chief doctor, the vice president of operations, and the vice president of customer relations to brainstorm some ideas. Their insights would probably include things like "We need to add more food options in the cafeteria" or "We should bring in some musicians to play music in the foyer."

Meanwhile, a hospital in the New Work Exchange would be more likely to assemble a nurse, someone in waste management, and a chaplain—because these are the people who interact with patients and spend the most time in treatment rooms. This group would be able to point out specific problems like "The paint is really dreary, and patients report it makes them feel depressed" or "The door hinges on bathroom doors all squeak." Stakeholders embedded in day-to-day interactions can create an immediate impact with their experience and knowledge.

Likewise, there are people inside our organizations who are 100 percent aware of the issues negatively impacting our businesses. Find them! Make them stakeholders in the business instead of relegating them to the side. Involve them in go teams. And then thank them—and reward them—for the results.

REMEMBERING TO FOCUS ON INCREMENTAL CHANGE

The adaptability paradox is real, so change must be handled incrementally. We can't do everything at once. Why not start by trying to improve 1 percent at a time? Incremental change is still change—and it's more realistic. The stages of change are such that the first few changes are always harder to achieve.

Workflows must be reset and protocols reconsidered across organizations, which takes time. It's important to differentiate between what's a marathon and what's a sprint. Both skills—and speeds—are required in the New Work Exchange.

While it takes time to gain speed, I also get pushback on the idea of picking up the pace. People say, "But Scott, if we speed things up too much, don't we risk getting sloppy and providing an inferior product or service?" Yes, that can be a problem. There are solutions to explore, including software that's faster, more automated, and able to work when teams are busy on other things. If you create a shoddy product or service, then you're actually slowing yourself down. So being aware of this potential problem should actually be motivation to explore options and solutions you haven't leveraged before. There are new platforms for everything every day—but also remember sometimes it's OK to start slow to get fast. Going slow is still faster than sitting still!

AUDITING OUR BUSINESSES AND OURSELVES

Ultimately, finding our pace requires us to identify where our organizations are falling behind. By assessing which organizational structures need to shift to meet the demand for immediacy, we're better positioned for *everything* in the New Work Exchange—including speed.

There are some hard questions we must all honestly process before we can really *make work better*. I've written these questions out in a manner that directs them toward organizations; however, with a few customizations, there are ways to apply these questions to *ourselves* as individuals. If people are the foundation of a new era of work, the change must start with us, regardless of our roles, positions, or ranks.

As such, I think of these questions as an audit to prepare us for the New Work Exchange:

- Are you willing to eliminate the formal hierarchy in your organization that's slowing down the decision-making process?

- Are you willing to trust your people and allow them to take more risks?

- Are you willing to push strategy further into the organization? Whether you do this through decentralizing decision-making or creating "go teams," what will this look like?

- Can you visualize a faster organization with automated systems that enable people to focus on more critical success factors?

SETTING A NEW PACE

Recently I stumbled across an interesting story about a company called Grab based in Southeast Asia. Like Uber, they provide rides and deliver food. As you might expect, Uber is their major competitor. When Grab decided to move into new territories, part of their strategy was to convince Uber drivers to switch over to work with them instead.

First, they tried the tech approach—they showed Uber drivers how their app was faster, had better GPS, and was more user friendly. But the response from the drivers was largely, "It's not *overwhelmingly* better, so I'm not going to move over to you guys."

Finally, the Grab team simply asked, "If the tech experience is essentially the same for you, then what *would* incentivize you to come over and work for us?" The question got right to the point. Drivers were clear. What they wanted more than anything was increased *frequency* in pay.

Grab listened. They created a system that issued drivers an ATM card. Each day a driver worked, pay would be transferred to the account associated with the card, making funds available for immediate use. As you can imagine, a lot of drivers decided to make the switch, and Grab now owns most of the market share in the area.

> Prioritizing people's needs and what matters to prospective team members can help businesses set a new pace, open new markets, and propel growth.

I want to end this chapter with this story because it illustrates an important point—sometimes finding our pace is less about the tools at our disposal and more about enabling true human communication. By asking the right questions, we're able to find *the rewards that matter to people.*

Let me repeat that for emphasis. Prioritizing people's needs and what matters to prospective team members can help businesses set a new pace, open new markets, and propel growth.

What if the Pony Express had tried to lease the land they needed access to from the local indigenous peoples rather than just attempting to claim it? Looking for common ground is generally a better way forward for everyone. Could the company have survived by fostering communication and trust, which would have facilitated their innovative methods to thrive? We'll never know.

But we can learn from change—even failed change—and apply it moving forward. With hindsight, we can try to avoid becoming another Blockbuster or Pony Express—market innovators that lost their way as the world around them changed.

Too often we *assume* what people want from work. We also assume that organizations, leaders, and managers know what we want or need from our work. It seems like such a simple thing, but communication—as challenging as we make it and as difficult as it sometimes feels—solves so many of our problems. Alignment is impossible without it. It's time to ask people what they need and want at work. Organizations need to listen and act on those priorities. And all of us need to grow the dialogue skills that enable us to better advocate for ourselves at work. To align, people *and* organizations must communicate priorities. Until we take those steps, speed is out of reach.

CONCLUDING IDEAS

Exchanging Old for New

O n August 8, 1588, an intense battle was waged off the coast of France that would forever shift the power dynamics of Europe. During what's now known as the Battle of Gravelines, England's naval forces surprisingly defeated the formidable Spanish Armada.

By all accounts, Spain's loss was the kind of upset that defied reason. Spain was arguably the most powerful country in the Western world at the time. Spain's King Philip II was part of the well-established Habsburg dynasty and son of Holy Roman Emperor Charles V. England, on the other hand, was small, isolated, and quite destitute after years of soap-opera-like royal drama, which had led to Elizabeth I ascending to the throne. At the time, the battle was seen as the strength and power of the Holy Roman Empire against *a woman*.

The Spanish Armada was massive in scope—a fleet of 130 heavy warships, some of them built just for invading England—and carried a whopping twenty-nine thousand men, most of them soldiers. In comparison, today's Spanish navy is made up of around twenty-one thousand total personnel, which should give you some idea of how big a deal it really was at the time.

Meanwhile, English forces consisted of two hundred smaller ships filled with sixteen thousand men—more civilian sailors rather than soldiers. Many people debated whether England's forces could even truly be considered a navy. Simply put, in terms of firepower, the odds in Las Vegas would've been on Spain.

So how'd the English win?

In short, their ships proved faster, both because of their smaller size and thanks to the expertise of England's seasoned sailors. When a severe storm erupted during early fighting, seamen at the helm of smaller ships with shallow construction found them easier to maneuver. Beyond this, the English were motivated by a single purpose: protecting their homeland.

With this united front, the English purposefully set fire to eight of their own ships and set them on a course for the larger, slower Spanish ships. The armada was forced to retreat from the resulting blaze, and after giving chase to the wounded armada, England sealed its victory.

In many ways, this battle from over four hundred years ago mirrors much of what we see happening today in the world of work. Where Spain emphasized the importance of a hierarchical military structure, England benefited from a nimbler force with smaller crews who could make quicker decisions. Where Spain was driven by top-down decisions, the English were motivated by a deeper purpose, which was empowered—not dictated—by their monarch.

As Mark Twain once put it, "History doesn't repeat itself, but it often rhymes."[59] As we set sail for the New Work Exchange, let's reflect: Which approach "rhymes" with your workplace? Are you the Spanish Armada? Or the English naval forces?

ACCEPTING THE ~~TIMES~~ WORKPLACES ARE A-CHANGIN'

We started out with one classic song reference, "Working for the Weekend," because it so embodies the mindset of workers who grind away in outdated and obsolete workplaces. So it only makes sense to bring us to a close with another classic song reference. Time to apply the ideas that inspired Bob Dylan's 1963 classic "The Times, They Are a-Changin'" to the work exchanges, old and new.

That's right: work and our workplaces are changing. Whether we like it or not, it's happening. Why not use that as an opportunity for alignment?

The New Work Exchange brings

That's right: work and our workplaces are changing. Whether we like it or not, it's happening. Why not use that as an opportunity for alignment?

unlimited possibilities to reset the system and move away from century-old concepts that disengage people from doing their best work. We'll still have problems, big and small, but perhaps we can use what we have learned from these changes to not only prepare for a better world in which to work but also to make the world a better place to work.

FOLLOWING THROUGH

Founded in 1919 as First Wisconsin Company, financial services firm Baird has been listed as one of Fortune's top 100 companies to work for nineteen consecutive years.[60] Having such a long history is commendable in its own right—being able to adapt with the times is even more so. As an employee-owned company, they realized a few years ago they needed to update their mission statement.

Their statement begins, "To provide the best financial advice and service to our clients ..." which still reflects the "clients first" approach established by the company's founder, Robert Baird. However, the second half of the statement demonstrates how organizational mission can balance internal and external stakeholders: "and be the best place to work for *our associates*." (Emphasis added.) They also created an associate promise statement that takes a strong person-centric position in saying, "We believe every associate matters."[61]

It could be easy to brush this aside as just nice words to put up on a wall, but again, they consistently rank as one of the best workplaces. Baird's reputation includes following up their promise—when something is off track, they not only fix it, but they include those impacted to help with the solutions.

Workplaces can't be simply performative. Following up and delivering on our promises—driving for impact and outcomes—must become our focus in the New Work Exchange.

Too many leaders *say* they want an organization or business to be a great place to work. Many even devote large portions of their time, energy, and budgets to attain such a status. Ultimately, though, it comes down to whether we *consistently follow through and act*. At the point of implementation, we often get stuck. As we've talked about, change comes with challenges and occurs in stages. That doesn't mean we should give up and embrace the adaptability paradox. It means we keep a learner's mindset, continue to ask important questions, and try again in new ways if necessary.

Cultural turnover requires change management. When we shift our perspectives, see colleagues as *people*, and then establish people as organizational stakeholders, we can set a new pace at work.

Good motives don't fix problems. Actions can. The sooner we act, the better. It's likely workplace changes will only increase over the next few years. Technology, environments, and circumstances will always impact work in ways that feel beyond our control. However, work will continue to play a major role in all of our lives, so finding ways to make it *better* is one of the most important things we can do as leaders, professionals, and as humans. The more proactive we are, the more prepared we will be as well.

So rather than bog us down with more concepts or homework, let's take the next step together by focusing on a specific question: What do we do next? Settling on where to start can be challenging, so here are a few ideas on how to take action and follow through.

TAKING INVENTORY OF PEOPLE EXPERIENCES

Set dedicated time aside to analyze your personal and organizational *people experiences* at work. Ask pointedly, "What am I (are we) doing to set people up for the fastest and highest levels of success?" Look at it from both the singular and plural perspective. How are *you* influencing and contributing to experiences? How can this adapt for the results you want to create? Then ask whether this is in alignment with organizational people experiences or whether there are things that need to shift. Can you influence those wider changes? Who can come alongside you to effect those changes?

Assess hiring processes and who's involved. Who writes job descriptions, and what's included? What are you asking candidates to do? Are team members involved and influential in the hiring process? Do existing team members influence who joins or even leads a team?

Dig into onboarding processes. What do people experience? Is it the bare minimum—knowledge and skills based? Is there opportunity for rapport building? Where are the opportunities to enrich the experience? If it's a digital process, what does that look like? How do people feel about it? How quickly does it enable success for the person at work?

The next area is significant: How are people rewarded for their contributions? Are people rewarded for the critical traits, skills, and behaviors that yield results? Are people rewarded for speed? How are people incentivized for epitomizing the specific values that are core to the organizational mission? What about incentives for growing the business? Are financial successes being shared with all those who influenced outcomes?

Finally, look at existing learning and development strategies. What tools and processes are in place for employee growth? How is performance evaluated? How is performance linked to growth strategy? Are people encouraged to learn new skills or prepare for new roles? Do performance outcomes align with goals?

When we consider things this way, it's possible to connect the dots between experiences. For example, you may discover the reason you're not seeing expected outcomes is because something significant isn't being covered in an onboarding process. Or perhaps job descriptions set unclear expectations. If you've got an eight-hundred-page employee manual, I can pretty much guarantee it's not digestible or setting people up for success, and that's going to show in your outcomes.

Answering these questions is essentially taking inventory of experiences people have across an organization. Yes, *write it all down*. Take the information and render the data or patterns in a way in which it can be shared and digested. When information is delivered visually, it's easier to communicate with others across a team.

When performing an experience inventory, there are some best practices to consider.

First, make the inventory immersive. Don't just sit in the office, reading through manuals and paperwork. Go through processes yourself, and invite team members to do so with you. Remember, we're building experiences. So go through onboarding, and role-play as a new hire. Construct a scenario, and have a leader or member of the C-suite do it with you. Go through the whole process from beginning to end—read the job description, apply for the job, and interview for the job. Take note of any bumps or difficulties. Then go through the onboarding process, and note what you liked and didn't like. Chances are that if something you experience is stale and disconnected from the mission, the same happens for new hires.

The second practice is to designate at least one real-life new hire for direct feedback. Let them know you're looking for any gaps in the process—and that you're looking for the problem areas, not compliments. If possible, get feedback from multiple new hires to get real and timely information. Be sure to signal and reinforce that the details of their experience are important. As helpful as it is to go through the process yourself, blind spots and gaps come from fresh perspectives. New people can see problems to which we've grown accustomed.

CHECKING THE SHELF LIFE

Ever thrown out something from your pantry past its expiration date? That can be done at work too. Checking the "shelf lives" of practices, policies, approaches, habits, and traditions in the workplace (in person and remote) is something we can all do more regularly.

What should that look like? For starters, assess the company mission statement and core values. Is it time for them to be updated? Or are there ones that need to be replaced entirely? When Baird updated their mission statement, it was because they realized the original had existed for one hundred years and needed to represent their existing and future workforce.

Missions and core values can appear timeless—an example is "Provide the best service"—but we shouldn't assume that they're working. Instead, try asking, "Is this adding enough value to our people?" Another good question to follow up with is, "Do we have the foundations to execute on those values?" In building a culture in which people are primary stakeholders, it's essential to have statements that resonate and connect with people. If a core value or mission statement isn't helping drive outcomes, then why keep it?

This approach extends to job descriptions too. Look closely at job descriptions to determine whether they reflect where your company is heading. Does the language across the descriptions consistently represent core values—or contradict them in any way? Are there ways to write descriptions to ensure they are usable and useful for the next three to five years?

Remember that while speed is important, there are different speeds for different tasks. Pace yourself. Nothing can or should be done all at once. Start with *one thing*, whatever is easiest, and then move on to the next item a month or two later. Gradual improvement is still an improvement. Taking an "all or nothing" approach is detrimental to long-term wins.

Look for ways to work with the existing timing and cycles within your organization. Start with what makes the most sense and take your time. Maybe it's easier to start with job descriptions if that's already part of your current work cycle. If discussing the mission statement is already scheduled, then start there. It's better to do it right at a cautious pace than to do a rush job that annoys everyone. This work should be meaningful and lead to outcomes; it should not be just another flash in the pan.

LISTING THE RULES

It's time to make a list of both your rules, written and unwritten.

The written rules are easy because they're probably already written down in manuals, process documents, and protocols. Consolidate anything that's a written rule. Audit documents and look for contradictions in message and execution. Do different teams abide by different rules? If so, why? Does the different nature of their work necessitate different rules? If so, then should they be referred to as guidelines instead to give people more optimal choices?

Beyond looking for contradictions, begin checking the "shelf life" on rules too. What rules have passed their expiration date and are just taking up space on the page? Are there rules that contradict the organization's mission or core values? Which rules are slowing things down and preventing productivity?

Compiling unwritten rules is more challenging but exceptionally important. Oftentimes our unwritten rules are more powerful than our written ones because they are shared between coworkers and not mandated in a company policy.

As we've taken this journey together, a few unwritten rules may have occurred to you. Those are great starts. Remember that we all have blind spots and habits. When we get used to things, we often don't notice them. This is where feedback from a new hire is worth its weight in gold. Another approach is to bring in outside help. So many organizations love helping companies uncover their unwritten rules and create change.

A best practice here with both the written and unwritten rules is to link actions to the statements—this is key for the impact capitalist. How are the rules impacting people? Are they helpful or unhelpful? Are they setting people up for success—or standing in the way of it?

This process often leads to discoveries. You may uncover rules that help the workplace. At Baird, they instituted the "No Asshole" policy. Yes, that's the real policy. They realized that if they were going to be a great place to work for associates, then a-holes couldn't be a part of the organization. So they wrote it down and put it into practice for how they do business, both internally and externally.

While this may sound like an outlier in a professional environment, that's the point when we create written rules. Rules should be more than statements—they should be linked to action. A rule like Baird's communicates, "If you're a jerk, you're not going to make it here." Then, as you might imagine, the company must follow through with actions such as a zero-tolerance approach to a-holes. Supporting *how* we do business is just as important as *whether* we do business— and creates a more positive culture for everyone.

IMAGINING WHAT IF ...

We can take away many lessons from the defeat of the Spanish Armada, but there are also a lot of "What if?" questions: "What if Philip II had used different ships? What if he had relied more on sailors who knew the sea instead of mostly soldiers? What if the Spanish soldiers had felt more aligned to the cause for which they were fighting?"

Too many companies are still trying to follow the Spanish Armada formula—top-down, hierarchical decision-making that treats "front line" people as a disposable means to an end. We can't know the answers to these "What if?" questions for sure, but history would've looked different—the world would've looked different. Decisions you make today will impact the future of work.

Some "What if?" questions lead to moments of reflection and regret. There are a time and a place for should've, would've, could've.

Wallowing in bittersweet regret can hold us back. Instead, we need to move forward. Our "What if?" questions exist to open the door to action. We audit, inventory, assess, and collaborate for the exciting possibility of a different future.

Everything we've discussed leads to a series of "What if?" questions. Such potential and opportunity with all those questions! What happens when we start implementing the answers to our questions and make changes? What if we start leading people instead of employees? What if we create policies and processes that set people up for unparalleled levels of success? What if the people within our businesses and organizations become our primary stakeholders?

Rules should be more than statements—they should be linked to action.

When we're asking these questions, what we're really asking becomes crystal clear: "What if we can make work better?"

I believe we can.

ACKNOWLEDGMENTS

My deepest gratitude to my colleagues at WorldatWork who continue to inspire and elevate the world at work!

An elevated, over-the-moon thank-you to Jonathan and Vanessa, who have helped this book come alive in so many unexpected ways.

Thank you, Christopher, for your unwavering support and unparalleled innovation, problem-solving, and creativity.

To Westley and Scooby-Doo, your support may have been mostly in your daily attempts to distract me with requests for more treats, walks, and bones, but in the end, you two were my writing pals, and I owe you big treats!

To Mihai, Cori, Marta, Sheetal, George, Mike, Courtney, and Elissa, thank you for seeing what is possible and charging after it to realize our vision of making the world a great place to work!

ABOUT WORLDATWORK

WorldatWork's mission is to improve the workplace by focusing on strategic rewards programs, equity, and human capital. For more than sixty-five years, we've helped organizations attract, motivate, and retain their most important capital—people. By connecting and educating those who cultivate inspired, engaged, productive, and committed employees in effective and rewarding work cultures, we influence people-centric workplaces. Strong organizational culture and work practices require strategic rewards programs coupled with a focus on fairness and equity.

Founded in 1955 as the American Compensation Association, WorldatWork is a member-driven association that helps business leaders, human resources professionals, and rewards practitioners in organizations of all sizes and in every industry globally. As the Total Rewards Association™, we also support our members (worldatwork.org/community) across the world who strive to make the world a better place to work.

WorldatWork's multimedia resources are intentionally designed to positively impact the working world.

PUBLICATIONS

WORLDATWORK.ORG/RESOURCES/PUBLICATIONS

Timely, practical, and insightful content written by leading experts, advisors, and journalists, providing cutting-edge information.

- Workspan

- #evolve

- Journal of Total Rewards

RESEARCH

WORLDATWORK.ORG/RESOURCES/RESEARCH

Fifty years of experience gathering and sharing data on the workplace, compensation, and rewards provide the insights and perspectives required to futureproof the workplace. Just-in-time pulse polling and research, coupled with annual surveys that document the state of work.

- 2022–2023 Salary Budget Survey

- Pay Equity Practices

- Compensation Programs and Practices

EDUCATION

WORLDATWORK.ORG/LEARN

Unparalleled courses, certifications, and webinars that address the top topics in the world of people management. Delivered as in-person, virtual, and on-demand learning options, our programs meet learners where they are on their career journeys.

- Certifications

  - ▫ Certified Compensation Professional / CCP®

  - ▫ Global Remuneration Professional / GRP®

  - ▫ Certified Benefits Professional / CBP®

  - ▫ Certified Executive Compensation Professional / CECP®

  - ▫ Certified Sales Compensation Professional / CSCP®

EVENTS

WORLDATWORK.ORG/CONFERENCES

Conferences and events built to suit the pressing needs of workplace leaders, influencers, and professionals. Network with thought leaders, subject matter experts, and renowned public speakers from across the globe at world-class events built to connect people and solve work's challenges.

- Rewards 2023

- Sales Comp 2023

- Rewards 2022 Highlights on Demand

ENDNOTES

1 Klaus Schwab, *The Fourth Industrial Revolution* (New York: Crown Business, 2016).

2 WorldatWork, "Workforce Planning in the Great Resignation Era," WorldatWork.org, March 2022, accessed October 17, 2022, https:// worldatwork.org/media/CDN/dist/CDN2/documents/pdf/resources/ research/WAW0522_Survey_WorkplacePlanning-FNL%20(1).pdf.

3 Kenneth W. Thomas, *Intrinsic Motivation at Work: What Really Drives Employee Engagement* (Oakland: Berrett-Koehler Publishers, 2000), ix.

4 Gallup, "State of the Global Workplace: 2022 Report," Annual Report (2022), https://www.gallup.com/workplace/349484/state-of-the-global-workplace.aspx.

5 Blair Heitmann, "Your Guide to Winning @ Work: Decoding the Sunday Scaries," LinkedIn.com, September 28, 2018, accessed September 28, 2022, https://blog.linkedin.com/2018/september/28/ your-guide-to-winning-work-decoding-the-sunday-scaries.

6 WorldatWork, "Why We Work: Drivers of Employer Choice and Employee Retention," WorldatWork.org, April 2021.

7   John F. Kennedy, "Kennedy Quotation," JFK Library.org, accessed September 26, 2022, https://www.jfklibrary.org/learn/about-jfk/life-of-john-f-kennedy/john-f-kennedy-quotations.

8   Association of American Railroads, "Chronology of America's Freight Railroads," accessed March 24, 2022, https://www.aar.org/chronology-of-americas-freight-railroads/.

9   Ed Catmull, *Creativity, Inc.: Overcoming the Unseen Forces That Stand in the Way of True Inspiration* (New York: Random House, 2014).

10   Marshall Goldsmith, *What Got You Here Won't Get You There* (London: Profile Books, 2008).

11   WorldatWork, "Total Rewards Inventory Programs and Practices, 2021," WorldatWork.org, October 2021.

12   Federal Reserve, "Employment Act of 1946," FederalReserveHistory.org, November 22, 2013, accessed October 18, 2022, https://www.federalreservehistory.org/essays/employment-act-of-1946.

13   Seren Morris, "McDonald's Restaurant Offers Free iPhones to Attract New Employees," Newsweek, May 24, 2021, https://www.newsweek.com/mcdonalds-restaurant-offers-free-iphones-attract-new-employees-1594143.

14   Kate Bernot, "Fast-Food Workers Can Now Be Paid Same-Day via Apps," The Takeout.com, May 20, 2019, accessed October 18, 2022, https://thetakeout.com/fast-food-workers-same-day-pay-apps-branch-instant-1834891419.

15   WorldatWork, "DEI Practices and Policies," WorldatWork.org, June 2021.

16   Rivka Mandelbaum, "Did Einstein Really Say That?." jGirls + Magazine, March 13, 2018, accessed September 7, 2022, https://jgirlsmagazine.org/2018/03/einstein-really-say/.

17 Jacqueline Brassey et al., "Future Proof: Solving the 'Adaptability Paradox' for the Long Term," McKinsey.com, August 2, 2021, accessed September 7, 2022, https://www.mckinsey.com/capabilities/people-and-organizational-performance/our-insights/future-proof-solving-the-adaptability-paradox-for-the-long-term.

18 WorldatWork, "Total Rewards Inventory Programs and Practices," WorldatWork.org, October 2021.

19 Matthew Boesler, "Profits Soar as Corporations Have Best Year Since 1950," Bloomberg, March 30, 2022, accessed October 18, 2022, https://www.bloomberg.com/news/articles/2022-03-30/2021-was-best-year-for-u-s-corporation-profits-since-1950.

20 Andrea Hsu, "How an Attendance Policy Brought the US to the Brink of a Nationwide Rail Strike," NPR.org, September 15, 2022, accessed October 18, 2022, https://www.npr.org/2022/09/14/1122918098/railroads-freight-rail-union-strike-train-workers.

21 Movement Mortgage, "About," Movement.com, accessed September 7, 2022, https://movement.com/about/.

22 Andy Warhol, "Andy Warhol Quotes," Brainyquote.com, accessed October 18, 2022, https://www.brainyquote.com/quotes/andy_warhol_395279.

23 Kenneth W. Thomas, *Intrinsic Motivation at Work: What Really Drives Employee Engagement* (Oakland: Berrett-Koehler Publishers, 2000), 11.

24 Gallup, "State of the Global Workplace: 2022 Report," Annual Report (2022), https://www.gallup.com/workplace/349484/state-of-the-global-workplace.aspx.

25 Ela Chodyniecka et al., "Money Can't Buy Your Employees' Loyalty," McKinsey.com, March 28, 2022, accessed October 18, 2022, https://www.mckinsey.com/capabilities/people-and-

organizational-performance/our-insights/the-organization-blog/
money-cant-buy-your-employees-loyalty.

26 Anne M. Mulcahy, "Motivation," StoryOfMulcahy.com, accessed October 18, 2022, https://storyofmulcahy.wordpress.com/motivation/.

27 Jeff Steen, "Pepsi's Former CEO Shared the 1-Sentence Secret to Her Success As a Leader: It's Opposite of What We've Been Told," Inc.com, October 6, 2021, accessed October 19, 2022, https://www.inc.com/ jeff-steen/pepsis-former-ceo-shared-1-sentence-secret-to-her-success-as-a-leader-its-opposite-of-what-weve-been-told.html.

28 Justin Bariso, "Netflix's Unlimited Vacation Policy Took Years to Get Right. It's a Lesson In Emotional Intelligence," Inc.com, accessed October 18, 2022, https://www.inc.com/justin-bariso/netflixs-unlim-ited-vacation-policy-took-years-to-get-right-its-a-lesson-in-emotional-intelligence.html.

29 WorldatWork, "Total Rewards Inventory Programs and Practices," WorldatWork.org, October, 2021.

30 Nu Yang, "More Employers Are Offering Sabbaticals To Prevent Employee Burnout," Workspan Daily, March 17, 2022, accessed October 19, 2022, https://worldatwork.org/resources/publications/ workspan-daily/more-employers-are-offering-sabbaticals-to-prevent-employee-burnout.

31 Unilever, "Future Workplace," Unilever.com, accessed October 18, 2022, https://www.unilever.com/planet-and-society/future-of-work/ future-workplace/.

32 Gabrielle Fonrouge, "Burger King Employee Who Didn't Miss a Day for 27 Years Gets $300K in Donations after Receiving Paltry Gifts," NYPost.com, July 1, 2022, accessed October 18, 2022, https://nypost. com/2022/07/01/burger-king-employee-who-didnt-miss-a-day-for-27-years-gets-300k-in-donations/.

33 ApprenticeshipUSA, "Our History," Apprenticeship.gov, accessed October 18, 2022, https://www.apprenticeship.gov/about-us/our-history.

34 Encyclopedia Britannica, "Eudaimonia," Britannica.com, accessed August 1, 2022, https://www.britannica.com/topic/eudaimonia.

35 WorldatWork, "Total Rewards Inventory Programs and Practices," WorldatWork.org, October, 2021.

36 Elizabeth Gulino, "Is Salary Transparency the Answer to Workplace Stress?," Refinery29.com, April 19, 2022, accessed October 18, 2022, https://www.refinery29.com/en-gb/benefits-salary-pay-transparency.

37 Syndio, "The 2023 Workplace Equity Trends Report: How HR, Total Rewards, and DE&I Leaders Are Approaching Pay Equity, Diversity, and Transparency," accessed October 18, 2022, https://synd.io/workplace-equity-trends-report/#pdf.

38 Amy Merrick, "Is the Friedman Doctrine Still Relevant in the 21st Century?," ChicagoBooth.edu, May 24, 2021, accessed October 18, 2022, https://www.chicagobooth.edu/review/friedman-doctrine-still-relevant-21st-century.

39 R. Edward Freeman, *Strategic Management: A Stakeholder Approach* (Cambridge, UK: Cambridge University Press, 1984), 5.

40 Jason Fernando, "What Are Stakeholders: Definition, Types, and Examples," Investopedia.com, June 29, 2022, accessed October 19, 2022, https://www.investopedia.com/terms/s/stakeholder.asp.

41 Business Roundtable, "Business Roundtable Redefines the Purpose of a Corporation to Promote 'An Economy That Serves All Americans,'" BusinessRoundtable.org, August 19, 2019, accessed October 19, 2022, https://www.businessroundtable.org/business-roundtable-redefines-the-purpose-of-a-corporation-to-promote-an-economy-that-serves-all-americans.

42   Becky Simon, "Stakeholder Theory and How Does it Impact an Organization?," Smartsheet.com, November 23, 2016, updated August 3, 2022, accessed October 19, 2022, https://www.smartsheet.com/what-stakeholder-theory-and-how-does-it-impact-organization.

43   National Center for Employee Ownership, "The Employee Ownership 100: America's Largest Employee-Owned Companies," NCEO.org, October 5, 2022, accessed October 19, 2022, https://www.nceo.org/articles/employee-ownership-100.

44   Jack Kelly, "Better.com's CEO Called Workers 'Dumb Dolphins'—Three Executives Quit," Forbes.com, December 8, 2021, accessed October 19, 2022, https://www.forbes.com/sites/jackkelly/2021/12/08/bettercoms-ceo-called-workers-dumb-dolphins-three-executives-quit/.

45   Abigail Johnson Hess, "'All Work Produces Value': What Experts Say Eric Adams Gets Wrong about 'Low Skill' Workers," CNBC.com, January 6, 2022, accessed October 19, 2022, https://www.cnbc.com/2022/01/06/what-experts-say-eric-adams-gets-wrong-about-low-skilled-workers.html.

46   US Bureau of Labor Statistics, "Employment by Major Industry Sector," BLS.gov, September 8, 2022, accessed October 19, 2022, https://www.bls.gov/emp/tables/employment-by-major-industry-sector.htm.

47   Marcus Buckingham and Curt Coffman, *First, Break All the Rules: What the World's Greatest Managers Do Differently* (Washington, DC: Gallup Press, 2005), 33.

48   Good Hire, "Warning to Managers: Survey Shows Most Workers Will Quit a Bad Boss," GoodHire.com, January 11, 2022, accessed October 19, 2022, https://www.goodhire.com/press-releases/warning-to-managers-survey-shows-most-workers-will-quit-a-bad-boss.

49   Lori Goler et al., "Why People Really Quit Their Jobs," *Harvard Business Review*, January 11, 2018, accessed October 19, 2022, https://hbr.org/2018/01/why-people-really-quit-their-jobs.

50 LinkedIn News, "Top Companies 2021: Atlanta," LinkedIn.com, July 27, 2021, accessed October 19, 2022, https://www.linkedin.com/pulse/top-companies-2021-atlanta-linkedin-news/.

51 Coca-Cola Europacific Partners, "Employer of Choice for a Fourth Consecutive Year," CocaColaEP.com, May 18, 2022, accessed October 19, 2022, https://www.cocacolaep.com/nz/news-and-insights/2022/employer-of-choice-for-a-fourth-consecutive-year/.

52 Cedric Luah, "Coca-Cola's Foray into the New Normal—Benefits, the Employee Experience and More," WTWco.com, November 10, 2021, accessed October 19, 2022, https://www.wtwco.com/en-IN/Insights/2021/11/coca-colas-foray-into-the-new-normal-benefits-the-employee-experience-and-more.

53 Tien Le, "Spanx CEO Surprises Every Employee with 2 First-Class Plane Tickets and $10,000," NPR.org, October 26, 2021, accessed October 19, 2022, https://www.npr.org/2021/10/26/1049340376/spanx-ceo-sara-blakely-first-class-plane-tickets-and-10000.

54 Evan Andrews, "10 Things You May Not Know about the Pony Express," History.com, June 3, 2016, updated August 29, 2018, accessed October 19, 2022, https://www.history.com/news/10-things-you-may-not-know-about-the-pony-express.

55 Graham Weaver, "How Walt Disney Demonstrated the Power of the '100/100 Rule'," GrahamWeaver.com, September 30, 2021, accessed October 19, 2022, https://www.grahamweaver.com/blog/walt-disney-100-100-rule.

56 Mark W. Denny, "Limits to Running Speed in Dogs, Horses and Humans," *Journal of Experimental Biology* 211, no. 24 (December 15, 2008): 3836–3849.

57 Jeré Longman, "Something Strange in Usain Bolt's Stride," The New York Times, July 20, 2017, accessed October 19, 2022, https://www.

nytimes.com/2017/07/20/sports/olympics/usain-bolt-stride-speed. html.

58   Eyder Peralta, "A Faster Human: Are We Unique In Our Ability To Get Better?," NPR.org, May 6, 2014, accessed October 19, 2022, https:// www.npr.org/sections/thetwo-way/2014/05/06/309839074/a-faster-human-are-we-unique-in-our-ability-to-get-better.

59   Christine Lagarde, "When History Rhymes," IMF.org, September 5, 2018, accessed October 19, 2022, https://www.imf.org/en/Blogs/ Articles/2018/11/05/blog-when-history-rhymes#.

60   Baird, "Baird Again Recognized among the Fortune 100 Best Companies to Work For," RWBaird.com, April 11, 2022, accessed October 19, 2022, https://www.rwbaird.com/newsroom/news/2022/04/baird-again-recognized-among-the-fortune-100-best-companies-to-work-for/.

61   Baird, "The Baird Difference," RWBaird.com, accessed October 19, 2022, https://www.rwbaird.com/bairddifference/ putting-the-best-work-for-you/best/.